Adeline Sergeant

Out of Due Season

A Mezzotint

Adeline Sergeant

Out of Due Season
A Mezzotint

ISBN/EAN: 9783744717861

Printed in Europe, USA, Canada, Australia, Japan

Cover: Foto ©Thomas Meinert / pixelio.de

More available books at **www.hansebooks.com**

OUT OF DUE SEASON

A MEZZOTINT

BY

ADELINE SERGEANT

AUTHOR OF

THE MISTRESS OF QUEST, THE STORY OF A PENITENT SOUL, ETC.

. . . "Spirits are not finely touched
But to fine issues" . . .

NEW YORK
D. APPLETON AND COMPANY
1895

OUT OF DUE SEASON.

I.

"Little, unremembered acts——"

It was a Saturday afternoon. In the sleepy
little town of Casterby there was not much done on
a Saturday afternoon in June. Many of the shops
in the High Street and the Market Place closed at
two. There was no business down at the yards and
the wharves on the river-side. The great arms of
the windmills had sunk into their Sabbath quietude.
The streets were deserted; but from the open doors
of every public-house came a buzz of tongues, a
clang of pewter-pots, a whiff of strong tobacco,
which showed that a fairly large number of the
male inhabitants of Casterby had betaken themselves to their favourite haunts and their favourite
occupation.

The younger men were out on the river, or play-

1

ing cricket in a flat green meadow outside the town, or loafing in groups at corners of the streets, with short pipes in their mouths. In one way or another they were amusing themselves. Their sisters and sweethearts were for the most part at home, lying on their beds in luxurious idleness, or putting the last touches to some bit of finery for the evening's wear. For after tea, by immemorial custom, the young men and maidens of Casterby went for a walk, generally in couples, to breathe the soft airs of hayfield, meadow, or river-bank, and to watch the moon rise and the stars come out over the level pasture-lands and the low-lying woods of Casterby Park.

Here and there, a youth sulked over his hard fate in having to keep watch and ward at his father's counter until six o'clock; or a conscientious girl submitted to the hand of destiny which had given her the charge of children or of a sick relation who could not be neglected; but for the most part, it was the tradition of Casterby that young people should have no sense of duty or obligation on a Saturday afternoon—that being the time appointed from all eternity for the relaxation of the body and the initiation of sexual relation-ships.

The little red town seemed to bask in the sun, lying in picturesque stillness on the banks of a placidly-flowing river, with wide flat meadows on either side, where rows of pollarded willows showed the dykes that divided the fields, and windmills stood up as the only landmarks in that waste of green against the cloudless sky. The fields melted into a blue haze of distance on the horizon, for there was not a hill within sight. The white road which entered one side of the town, crossed the bridge and ran through the Market Place—losing itself for a time in a stretch of cobble-stones, and emerging on the other side between green hedges on its way into the vast unknown—this white and dusty road had no fatiguing ups and downs for many a long mile, but meandered flatly onward in uniform monotony. It might have been taken as a figure of many a life in the little town of Casterby—a life where there was no obstacle and much uniformity, but where the objects of interest were few and far between, and the out-look on either side the road very much restricted.

But there were also by-ways of a more alluring kind.

It was in the families of middle-class tradesfolk and small professional men that this monotony was mostly to be found. The rich lawyer and the popular doctor, living outside the town, had resources and diversions which the shop-people did not dream of. The parson had his church and his charities. The Squire—represented by Mr. Lisle of the Court —was often in London or in "foreign parts," and, being a Roman Catholic, held himself a little apart from the other magnates of the county and the institutions of the town. In these men's houses, dimly represented to the Casterby people by a stack of chimneys seen between clumps of stately trees, or a garden-wall, draped with Virginian creeper, from behind which came sounds of laughter and song and the echo of strange outlandish games, it seemed almost to the homely folk outside as if an alien people dwelt. Doubtless, to the Lisle girls and their neighbours, the young Collingwoods of Areke, shut in by the great park gates, and scarcely conscious of anything unbeautiful in the world, the lives of people who lived behind shops and counting-houses were just as inconceivable.

And there was also another class in Casterby where life was anything but monotonous. Small as the town was, it had its low-lying tangled slums, where a crowd of labourers, mostly Irish and Roman Catholics, herded with their wives and children in squalid little red-brick houses, and passed their time in an alternation of toil at the brickfields and drunken revelry at the public-house.

The fact that Mr. Lisle was a Roman Catholic, and that there was a neat little Romanist chapel in Casterby, helped to attract this class of labourers to the place; and apart from them there was also a contingent of ordinary drunken Englishmen, who were even more difficult to manage than the Irish labourers. Far removed from the stolid respectability of the trading folk, further still from the careful refinements of the Court, there flourished in the back-streets of Casterby as much vice and misery, disease and dirt, as could well be found in a town that did not number quite three thousand inhabitants upon the census-roll.

The beams of the warm June sun, shining

through the dusty panes of a carpenter's workshop, struck full on the face and figure of Gideon Blake, as, with heavily frowning brow, he handled plane and saw as though his life depended on the amount of labour he could accomplish, that sleepy Saturday afternoon. Not that he worked with any appearance of ardour. It was simply that he did not raise his eyes or take his attention from his occupation for a moment; he toiled with a certain grimness and pertinacity of purpose not often seen in a lad of his age. For he was not more than twenty years old, although at first sight he seemed older. His height and his breadth of chest and shoulders were remarkable; his muscles and sinews were of iron; one would have said (but it would not have been true) that his nerves were of steel. His forehead was broad, and well developed above the deep-set dark eyes; his jaw a little too massive for the line of beauty. His mouth possessed some curiously sensitive curves, which struck one as out of place in that strong face; but it was not a good mouth for all that. It was sullen in repose, with a droop at the corners which betokened discontent. For the rest, his face was well featured, and when he raised himself from his stooping posture it could be seen that his somewhat gaunt frame had in it the makings of a giant. In stooping, the thing most noticeable about him was the great arch of his head, where a phrenologist would have said that the qualities of veneration and benevolence predominated. Those who knew Gideon Blake would, however, have laughed this verdict to scorn. He did not bear an amiable character in Casterby.

At last a shadow fell between him and the sun. He took no notice of it for some time; then he raised himself, shook the mass of heavy black hair out of his eyes. and looked threateningly at the intruder, who was a spare, middle-sized man with scant gray hair and whiskers, a face mottled by long exposure to wind and weather, a clear, shrewd, gray-blue eye, and a peculiarly long upper-lip. His waistcoat was generally remarked on by strangers, as it was of a stout serviceable silk, with a pattern of red and blue, now much confused in colouring by the lapse of time and the stains of beer and tobacco; but it was an article of attire that Obed Pilcher was proud of.

"A bit owd-fashioned," he had been heard to

say, as he looked down at it complacently, "but noan the wuss for that. It's allus better to get a good stooff at beginning, an' stick to 't. Owd Squoire gi'e me this, a' did, an' it'll last ma toime."

It had, in fact, once been a handsome garment of flowered silk, worn by the old Squire himself, in days when stiff flowered waistcoats were fashionable, and to Obed's eyes it was as good as ever. His trousers were of ordinary gray, usually turned up at the ankles (on week-days) to show an inch of blue stocking, but his coat was always of a rusty black. On Sundays he blossomed forth in a complete suit of sables, these being usually the Vicar's gift; for Obed Pilcher was parish clerk and verger, or "pew-opener," as he called it, at the parish church. He magnified his office; on the whole, he considered himself more important in Casterby church than any other functionary. Vicars might change and curates come and go, but the parish clerk remained in his glory until the day of death.

Mr. Pilcher was the brother of Gideon Blake's mother, who had died at his birth. It was perhaps on account of her early death that he had an especial, although somewhat sneaking, affection for his

nephew. Not that he showed it in words, scarcely
in deeds; but it was noticed that whenever Gideon
was in trouble or disgrace, Obed Pilcher made a
point of seeking him out and giving him his society,
often for two or three hours at a stretch, without
offering a reason and without trying to converse.
Gideon betrayed no pleasure at these visits, but
also little or no impatience. It might have been
conjectured that he was not aware of their signifi-
cance; but Gideon Blake often saw more than he
chose to show, and he by no means wore his heart
upon his sleeve.

On this occasion he eyed his visitor angrily, and
said:

"Well?"

Obed nodded in reply.

"Good-day t' ye, Gideon. Main hot weather,
bain't it?"

Gideon seemed to think it not worth while to
respond. He crossed his brown arms over his
broad breast, and leaned back against the wall,
turning his handsome, sullen face a little to one
side. Obed moved restlessly from one foot to another, then felt in his pocket for his snuff-box, and

deliberately took a pinch of snuff between his finger and thumb.

"Emmy's at hoame," he said, looking at the snuff-box. "At hoame, doin' nowt. Ah saw Emmy as ah coom by."

No answer. But a dull red colour crept slowly into Gideon's face, and a mute anger showed itself in his dark eyes.

"Emmy's well enough. She bain't a bad lass, Emmy. She doan't mean nowt. But she's stunt. All the Enderbys is stunt. Dunnot think the wuss of her for that."

"I don't," said Gideon sharply.

His uncle took the long-suspended pinch of snuff, and sneezed two or three times with portentous solemnity, as if he wished to give his nephew time to consider his words. But Gideon said no more.

"Eh, well. It's a rare noight for t' watter. Thee be goin' along o' Mortlock's party, ah reckon?"

"What business is it o' yours?" said Gideon, moving from the wall and looking round for his coat. "I'm going nowhere to-night."

"*She's* not goin' in Mortlock's boat?"

"Not she. No party for her. She's got a chap of her own, and a boat too, all to themselves."

And Gideon flung himself angrily into his jacket.

"Ay, ay," said Obed slowly. "Ah thowt as mooch. Young Chiltern, I lay, from Hull. The lasses is all agate after him."

Gideon muttered a savage curse on young Chiltern, which Mr. Pilcher, as the parish clerk, affected not to hear.

"Dinna fash thasen', Gideon. Th' lass is all right. She'll not tak' oop wi' trash like Chiltern, for all his goold chaains an' rings. She knaws a mon when she sees un, Emmy does."

Gideon was resolved against being comforted, but, in spite of himself, his face cleared a little.

"She may take Chiltern, for all I care," he said obstinately; "but if she takes him, she don't get me too—that's all."

To nobody else in Casterby would he have said as much.

Obed Pilcher shook his head.

"Emmy's a foine strapping lass," he said sagaciously. "An' a fine strapping lass mun tak' her bit o' foon. It's foon, lad, foon—nowt else."

"She'll have to choose between her fun—and me," said Gideon.

Then he stepped out of the shed, and stood for a moment in the blaze of the afternoon sun, his hands in his pockets, his angry eyes fixed on the ground.

"Come for a turn wi' me," said Obed persuasively.

"Well, maybe I will." But he looked irresolute, and did not walk very quickly towards the gate.

The Blakes' house, a square red-brick block two stories high, with stiff white windows and prim painted doors, stood just outside the wood-yard. It fronted the road, with a small garden before it, and a flagged walk from the front-door to the gate; and the long narrow back-garden ran past the yard, divided from it only by a low privet hedge. A white gate, of considerable width and height, opened on the road from the wood-yard; but when Gideon Blake's father and his family came to and from the house to the yard, they generally walked through a gap in the privet hedge, without troubling themselves about gates. Gideon was, however, making for the highroad, when a girl about twelve ran out at the back-door and stood on the garden side of the hedge, shaking her short skirts and calling to him :

"Gid! Gid! Tea's ready. You're to bring Uncle Obed in to tea."

Gideon looked at his uncle, and turned passively towards the house. Uncle Obed nodded and spoke to the child who was dancing on the gravelled path as if she did not know how to keep her feet still.

"I'm going on Mortlock's boat," she screamed out, as they approached. "Dad says I may. We shan't get home till midnight. All the Shipton girls are going, too."

"Mortlock's boat" was a pleasure-barge, often hired on a Saturday evening by some dozen or twenty young people of Casterby for an excursion down the river. Staid and sober-going folk had their objections to these Saturday parties, for they were not without a rowdy element, although supposed to be conducted on respectable lines. There was usually a good deal of chorus-singing, and a great supply of beer ; the young men sat with their arms round the waists of the girls of their choice, and there was more kissing than would have been deemed decorous in conventional circles.

Gideon took no notice of his stepsister's announcement, at which Uncle Obed wagged his head solemnly.

" A lile lass like you," he said, "mout be better in her bed, ready for Sunday."

Carry Blake laughed scornfully, and pirouetted on one foot towards the house.

" I'm going to enjoy myself. I'm not always in the sulks, like Gideon," she called over her shoulder in reply.

She looked as if she might some day develop into a pretty girl, for she had long fair hair, eyes of speedwell blue, and a red-and-white complexion ; but her features were curiously thin and sharp, and the meagre-lipped, wide mouth showed two rows of large white teeth which seemed out of proportion to her size. She was the elder child of Joseph Blake's second wife.

Gideon and Obed followed her through the back-door and into the little sitting-room where

the tea-table was laid. For Mrs. Blake held herself high above the vulgarity of sitting in the
kitchen, as Joe Blake had always done before she
married him.

"Good enough to smoke in—good enough for
you and your *Pilchers!*" she had often exclaimed,
with an acidulated emphasis upon the maiden name
of Gideon's mother; "but *my* father had one of the
first drapery establishments in Gainsborough, and
we had never anything to do with common labourers——"

Which was an unkind skit at Gideon's mother,
whose father had been a small tenant-farmer who
had come down in the world through inability to
pay his rent.

Mrs. Blake prided herself on her "genteel" appearance, as well as her distinguished parentage.
She was a tall, spare woman, in whom one saw her
daughter's face grown old. There were the same
sharp features, accentuated by age; the same blue
eyes, grown paler and with reddened lids; the same
almost lipless mouth, and big teeth which were no
longer white, but yellow, tusk-like, and ferocious.
Not that Mrs. Blake gave one the impression of

ferocity ; but that she was possessed of some genuine spitefulness there could be but little doubt. She was always civil to Obed Pilcher in his presence, but she had as little love for him as for Gideon, or for the dead woman in whose place she sat.

She was dressed rather smartly, in a green gown, with a wide and very unbecoming fichu of real lace round her neck. She always wore smarter and more expensive things than were quite suitable to her position, because she got them at wholesale prices from her father's shop. Carry also was over-dressed, and many people wondered how "poor Joe Blake" could afford such extravagance, and why he did not put a stop to it. As if poor Joe Blake could ever have put a stop to anything that his wife desired !

He was sitting at the tea-table when his brother-in-law came in, and turned to greet him with hearty kindliness.

" Well, Obed, how goes the world with you ? Come in, come in ; draw up a chair, and take a cup o' tea. Mother's all in her throngs to-day, but she's as glad to see you as I am."

" Certainly, Mr. Pilcher," said Mrs. Blake.

"Pray sit down; and Gideon, too, if he's going to stay."

"Why shouldn't he stay?" said Joe Blake mildly, as if he noted something peculiar in his wife's tone. He was large and dark, as Gideon was; but there was none of Gideon's strenuous gloom in his placid countenance. Only an easy-going man could have kept the peace as he did, between a fault-finding second wife and an irascible grown-up son, who were generally at daggers drawn.

Gideon frowned, and Carry burst out laughing.

"Why, dad," she said, "he's generally out with Emmy Enderby on a Saturday afternoon. Don't you know that?"

"Emily Enderby is wiser than I took her for," said Mrs. Blake's exasperating voice. "She knows the value of two strings to her bow."

"Ah saw Emmy Enderby as ah come by," said Obed Pilcher, his broad accent causing Mrs. Blake to shiver with affected horror at the sound. "She was just sitting along of her mother, sewing of a gownd."

If he had expected to throw oil on the troubled waters, he was disappointed. Carry's shrill laughter and shriller tones rang unmusically through the room.

"Her frock—her new frock for to-night!" she cried. "Uncle Obed, that's just the fun. She's going out with Mr. Fred Chiltern, from Hull: he's to row her up to Farmby, and have supper at the inn with the Mortlock party—that's what Emmy Enderby's going to do. I shall see her. Gideon, why don't you come, too?"

There was a curious change in Gideon's face; it had turned pale, not red, and his lips were stern. He was still standing near the door; the others were seated, and Carry turned laughing eyes upon him from over the back of her chair.

"The fam'ly's back at t' Park," said Obed, by way of changing the conversation; and Joe Blake grunted a sociable interest in the news. But the women of the family could not let Emmy Enderby's doings pass without further criticism.

"If she gets Fred Chiltern, she'll do very well," said Mrs. Blake. "He has a very good position, I hear. He's foreman already, and they say he'll be a partner by and by. He has real nice manners, too—so amiable and obliging—which is more than can be said of *all* young men."

"I expect they'll come back engaged," said Carry, giggling in Gideon's face. "Shall you be sorry, Gid?"

"You'll be sorry soon that you can't hold your tongue," replied her stepbrother grimly.

"I'll tell Emmy you said so! I'll tell her how cross you were! I'll tell her—oh! oh! Ma, make him leave off!" For Gideon had seized her by the shoulders with no gentle hands.

"How dare you touch my child? You brute! Why don't you speak to him, Joseph? Carry, you shouldn't tease! Gideon, for goodness' sake! don't sit down with us if you can't keep your temper."

"I don't mean to," said Gideon, upon whom Mrs. Blake's tempest of scolding words fell with very little effect. "I only wish I had never to sit down with that little vixen any more."

"Gid! Gid!" muttered the mild-natured father.

But Gideon did not hear. He strode out of the room and banged the door behind him, like the ill-conditioned, unmannerly boy that he was.

And Mrs. Blake scolded her husband in place of him for the rest of the meal.

Obed Pilcher and his brother-in-law retired to a garden bench shortly afterwards, to smoke their long clay pipes in peace. Joe Blake was not much disturbed in his mind, but Obed was uneasy.

"That boy o' yourn——" he said at last, with difficulty.

"Eh?" said Joe.

"He be maain soft on Emmy Enderby."

"He be main cranky-tempered," said Gideon's father with serenity. "I often thinks to myself, if I'd ha' laid the strap on him a bit oftener when he was small, he'd ha' been easier to deal with now. My missis often told me so, but I allers said I didn't hold wi' too much flogging."

"He wouldn't ha' stood it," said Obed; "he'd ha' run away to sea, or summat. The lad's got mettle. 'Faythers, provoke not your children to wrath,' is Scripter words."

"Ay, but there's another text of a different bearin'," said Joe doubtfully: "'Spare the rod an' spile the child,' eh? It's what Lavinia's been quoting to me ever since Gideon was *that* high."

"Wimmin doan't understand men-folk, nor yet boys," said Obed. "Least of all Gideon. She'd ha' drove him out o' Casterby years ago, if she'd had the fettlin' of him. Ah doan't know where he gets his sperit from. It bain't *you*, Joe, nor was it poor Ruth; an' ah'm blessed," he added reflectively, "if a' gets it from *me*."

"Ay, you was allers a quiet sort o' chap, Obed," said Joe. "But though Gid mayn't get his sperit from me, yet 'tis from my side o' t' house it springs from. There was an uncle o' mine as was the same sperity, high-stummicked sort o' chap. He ran away from hoame, an' were lost at sea. They did say as he took after his grandf'er, who was just such another; an' that's, mebbe, where Gideon gets his temper from, for they say it runs in fam'lies sometimes—like rheumatics."

"Ah've heard that the Blakes was a terrible wild lot," said Obed. "It 'ud never do to be too hard on Gid, Joe."

"Well, I beain't hard on 'im; it's the missus, not me. An' at Gid's age, she can't hurt him much."

"Ah've bin thinkin'," said Obed, with natural

hesitation—"ah've bin thinkin' he'll want to be married afore long."

"Ay, Emmy Enderby—if she'll have him. But they're ower-young yet."

"He's close on one-an'-twenty. Ah've bin thinkin'——"

"Well, Obed?"

"Ah've gotten more rooms i' ma hoose than ah've any use for, Joe. If Gideon an' Emmy was to coom, it 'ud be main an' cheerful for me."

"What—*live* with you?" said Blake, laying down his pipe and looking at Obed with perplexed interest. "Gid and Emmy?"

Mr. Pilcher nodded a solemn assent.

"Gid's not—well, *easy* to live with, Obed."

"Ah knows Gid very well," said the parish clerk, nodding his head.

"Have you asked him what he thinks of the plan?"

"Nay."

"Emmy mayn't like it, ye see. I don't know, nayther, if she means to take him or not."

"She'll take un," said Obed with decision.

" An'—sithee, she'll take un all the sooner if he's got an house to put her in."

" A—ay," said Joe Blake, with lengthened intonation. " But Emmy's high in her notions. The Enderbys was allers high."

" Ah'm 'igh, too," said Obed stolidly.

And Joe beat his pipe meditatively against his hand, and wondered whether Obed had saved money.

" Then," he said presently, " there's church."

" Ay," said Obed, " there's church, plaain eno'; what o' that? Gideon bean't chapel; nor Enderbys nayther."

" No," said Joe, with meaning, " an' I ain't chapel, nayther; but Gideon's nowt. I don't hold wi' folk allers runnin' off to meetin', as chapel folks does; but I likes 'em to go Christmas an' Easter, an' now an' then of a Sunday. But Gideon's turned against it ever since he was twelve year old, and not all the larrupin' in the world ever served to get him back since the day when parson boxed him after service because he'd made a noise during psalms."

" Ay, owd parson loikes to gie the boys a knock

now an' then," said Obed, with perfect equanimity.
" They mostly desarves it. But he be too owd an'
blind to ha' done much i' that way lately."

" But that won't make Gid go to church any the
more. An' to my thinking, Obed, it be a trifle unbecoming that you, being parish clerk, should take
to live wi' you a young man as never passes the
threshold. Parson 'll take it as a reflection on his-
self, and be put out; and, for my part," said Joe
Blake slowly and wisely, " I don't hold wi' offend-
ing folk, in partick'lar the quality."

" Thee can leave such matters to me, Joseph
Blake," said Obed, with a grand wave of his hand.
" Ah know what ah'm doin', as well as most foalk.
Wheer t' wife goes, husband goes, an' no question
asked. Emmy ain't one as 'll be satisfied wi'out
showin' her new ribbons in church, nor her new
husband, and Gid 'll be like wax in them pretty
fingers of hern. Doan't thee think thasen so wise,
Joe."

" Well, mebbe you're right," said Joe. Then
he stood up and looked into the distance, with a
softer light in his deep-set dark eyes. " Ah'm not
one to trouble the church much," he said, " but I

sometimes think Ruth 'ud be vexed to see the lad so set against it—an' you the parish clerk an' all. So do as you like, Obed Pilcher—do as you like."

"Ah mun be gooin,'" said Obed. "Ah'll mebbe see the lad to-night, an' cheer un up wi' the news. He's a bit downcast now, but it'll be all right when young Chiltern's gone back to Hull."

He took his leave, and marched off in search of his nephew.

But Gideon was nowhere to be found.

II.

" The God of Love—ah, benedicite ! "

OBED did not find his nephew, because Gideon had haunts of his own where no other foot ever penetrated. Over the workshop there was a low, dark garret, a mere hole beneath the eaves, which the lad had made into a den for himself. It showed his unlikeness to his compeers in Casterby that he should ever have conceived the desire of a hiding-place. The average youth dislikes to be alone. But a certain amount of loneliness was to Gideon as the breath of life.

His chamber had a sloping roof for a wall, and was barely six feet in breadth, although of considerable length, as it extended the whole length of the workshop. It had once been open to wind and rain, but Gideon had stealthily filled in the side with boards, and had then contrived to fasten a

pane of glass into them for the sake of light. At
first this had been enough for him; but after a
time he put in a latticed window with hinges, so
that he could get air as well as light. For, as it
happened, there was an excellent view of the
meadows and the river from Gideon's glory-hole,
and he had grown, without knowing why, to love
it. Sometimes, when no one knew what had become of him, and even his father suspected that he
was engaged in mere mischief-making, he was
lying at full length under the eaves, with chin
pillowed by his hands, gazing out at the sunlit
fields, at the clear shimmering line of the river, at
the thousand and one changes produced by light
and shade in the landscape, which he seemed to
know by heart, yet never knew well enough. He
could barely stand upright in his garret, but he
could lie down and gaze out of the window, or he
could sit and read. He was not much of a reader,
however; he liked better to watch the sky, or to
use his hands in the carving of wood to shapes
which had more artistic value than he knew. Few
persons knew of his skill in this respect. He
carved things for the pleasure it gave him, not for

sale or show. There was a walking-stick, rich in grotesques, which he meant one day for Obed Pilcher; a work-box, entwined with creeping stems and flowers and fruit, for Emmy Enderby; a picture-frame, designed to hold a hideous black outline of his mother's head—the only likeness he had of her—for his father; but as yet he had never summoned up courage to give any of these things to their rightful owners. He felt a certain shyness about it. And very likely nobody would care for his work, after all. So he said to himself in moments of depression, which with him were not rare.

He had not a happy disposition. He could not take things easily as others did. Life seemed hard to him. He had known little love, and love was the only thing that would have sweetened his temper and softened his self-will. He was believed by his stepmother to have no feeling; but in reality every one of her harsh words made him suffer acutely. He did not doubt that all she said was true. He was morose, selfish, violent, domineering, even brutal—people said so, and that was enough. It made him worse to know the character that his little world gave him; in his dark moods he used to resolve to be as bad as his stepmother believed him. Even his father had no faith in him, although he was kind enough. The only person who trusted him through thick and thin was his uncle, Obed Pilcher. And Gideon loved him for it in his heart.

It was not easy to get on with Gideon, certainly. His hand was against every man's, and every man's hand against his. He had a sullen, ungovernable temper, and a habit of brooding melancholy which was often mistaken for sullenness. And he was very ignorant. He had refused to go to school after he was twelve years old, and at the same age, as his father had said, he had also rebelled against church. Casterby was neither a scholarly nor a church-going place; nevertheless, Gideon's revolt was unprecedented, and caused him to be set down as a black sheep. Careful mothers kept their children away from him; strict fathers forbade their sons to make him their friend. They did not care about religion themselves; but it was not respectable never to be seen at church. Thus Gideon was an Ishmael at a very early age, and

3

had an evil reputation which was hardly warranted by his deeds.

It is many years since Gideon Blake was young, and Casterby is a changed place nowadays. Its grammar-school is becoming famous; its church is ritualistic and "advanced"; it is rather proud of its sanitary condition, its electric lighting, its shady side-walks. But in those days the grammar-school had barely half a dozen pupils, taught by an inefficient old man, who ultimately drank himself to death; and the empty church was a desolate place, where the congregation made use of the altar-table and the font as convenient resting-places for their hats, and the clerk read the responses from the lowest tier of a "three-decker"; and the streets were paved with cobble-stones, and the back lanes were a disgrace to civilization. What wonder, then, if Gideon Blake's mental powers and moral nature were allowed to run wild, and his nobler instincts to die down without a struggle, because no one cared whether his soul were alive or dead?

But the finer the nature, the more keenly it suffers when starved in this way. Gideon did not know why he suffered, but now and then he was conscious of a desperate intolerance of his lot. He wanted something, and he could not put his longing into words. The wonder was that his impatience had not driven him forth into the world, to find out what was wrong with himself and his life. But he was withheld for two reasons. One was his silent affection for his uncle, Obed Pilcher, to whom he knew himself to be the centre of existence. The other reason was one of temperament. With all his impatience and rebellion of spirit, he had the habit of dumb endurance, which had, perhaps, descended to him through generations of peasant fore-fathers—the reticence, the passivity of men of the soil. He could feel, suffer, endure; he hardly knew how to take the initiative in freeing himself from bonds.

His one solace lay in that window in the garret, which was to him like a window of the soul. He had strange thoughts of life and death, of God and of eternity, as he lay and watched the passing of the clouds, the shining of the sun by day, the great procession of the stars by night. He could not have put them into words to save his life, and yet they made him different from the ordinary bucolic youth—they set a barrier between him and the shop-lads who measured ribbons at noon, and pursued questionable recreations when the shop was shut. They made him vaguely contemptuous of the ordinary occupations and interests of his kind, yet they supplied him with no definite interests or objects of his own. Many an observer would have judged these long solitary musings as things that did harm rather than good.

And yet, finer issues might be hoped for, when the spirit was so finely touched by things that pertained to heaven rather than to earth.

Into this sad-coloured, self-centred life there came quite suddenly that blossoming of the whole being which goes by the name of love.

"Emmy Enderby!" How often he had said the simple little name to himself! He had carved it with a hundred different flourishes and designs all over the walls of his room. He had dreamed of her night and day ever since she first took his fancy captive; he had lost the memory of his old aspirations—if the vague thoughts of his future could be dignified by that name—henceforth he

lived only for her. It was a passion of unusual
intensity in one so young, a tropical passion, almost
unknown in the green wastes of Casterby, where
love was rated for the most part as a matter for
mingled jocosity and shame. Gideon was not
ashamed of his love, nor inclined to make a joke
of it. He would have proclaimed it—rudely and
fiercely, perhaps—to all the world, if he could. It
was a fire that consumed him—a sacred flame.

He had known Emmy Enderby since she was a
child; but he had never noticed her until her return
from the cheap boarding-school to which she had
been sent for a couple of years by her proud parents.
Proud they were of her beauty, of her cleverness,
and willing to make sacrifices for her sake. Her
father was only an ironmonger, though for some
years a successful one, and he did not set himself up
to rank with Mr. Blake, who had a wood-yard and
a flourishing business and a good many workmen
under him. Such fine distinctions would have been
almost incomprehensible to the minds of the Rector's
family or the Lisles; they would have classed the
Blakes and the Enderbys together as tradespeople,
and seen no difference. But there was all the

difference in the world in Casterby eyes; for James
Enderby kept a mere shop, while Joseph Blake
ranked as a wholesale dealer and supplied "the
trade."

Moreover, Enderby had come down in the world.
He had failed once, and was now doing business "in
a very small way." But Emmy, six months home
from school, and barely eighteen, was unaffected by
her father's troubles, and amused herself all day long
to the best of her ability, while her mother toiled at
household matters and the management of a large
family. Emmy certainly toiled not, neither did she
spin. She felt herself too pretty and too superior
to work; and the girls at school had told her that
she was sure to be married before she was nineteen.
Emmy thought that she would like to be married—
and she also liked Gideon Blake. She was not
formally "engaged" to him, but she knew that she
might be whenever she chose.

Her liking of him, however, did not restrain her
from flirting with any man who made advances to
her. All the more had she done this since she had
discovered that her flirtations drove Gideon into a
frenzy of jealousy. It amused her to see her power

over him, and it was not in her nature to understand the suffering which she inflicted. Perhaps she
would not have cared much, if she had understood.

Up in the little room beneath the roof, Gideon
waited and watched. He was undergoing a silent
agony of wounded feeling. He writhed with pain as
he pictured the scenes in which Emmy was moving:
he saw her helped into the barge by Fred Chiltern's
hand; sitting close to Fred Chiltern, perhaps with
his arm round her waist when darkness began to
fall; allowing him to kiss her, perhaps, when they
said good-bye. At that moment he loathed Fred
Chiltern—hitherto known to him as a dapper, self-
satisfied harmless little draper's assistant, whom he
had considered as a person of no account whatever—
loathed and hated him with a passionate hatred
which turned him giddy and sick with its vehemence. But he did not move; he lay motionless,
watching the golden afternoon glide into the mel-
lower evening light, and the shadows of the poplar
trees in the hedges grow so long that they stretched
half across the meadows, and the clear waters of the
winding river turn red here and there as if they
were tinged with blood. It was not until the

colour had begun to die out of the landscape, and a light haze to show itself across the fields, that he roused himself from his crouching position, and, after some consideration, crept down the ladder which gave access to his garret, and made his way into the street.

His father's house and yard were not on the highroad, but on one that crossed the main street of Casterby at right angles—a by-way, leading to nowhere in particular, losing itself in a narrow lane and a stretch of fields at the further end. But two minutes' walk brought Gideon to the street of red-brick irregular houses, here beginning to look less crowded together than in the centre of the town, for the Blakes' side-street was near the outskirts of Casterby, leading from the uninteresting white road that crept away from the red houses to its course between the fields. Gideon did not turn to the left hand, which would have led him out of the town. He faced to the right, and swung down towards the Market Place and the river.

The shops were shut, and the twilight of a June day was closing in. Very few persons were in the streets. There was a little group round the steps of

the Independent chapel, the little red-brick building near Dane Street (the by-road in which Joseph
Blake lived); but Gideon avoided it by passing on
the other side. After crossing the road, he passed
close by the open gate of the Roman Catholic
chapel—places of worship were thick in Casterby—
and he gave a glance of contempt and disgust at
the building as he went by. He had no particular
love for his own form of religious faith, but he had
been brought up to despise all others. Yet he was
not without a kind of sneaking curiosity to know
what went on inside the place which he had heard
vaguely and inaccurately described as "the very
gate of hell." If there was not much religion,
there was a good deal of theological bitterness in
Casterby. A glimpse of lighted candles, a whiff of
stale incense, seen and felt now and then as he hurried by, had always produced a peculiarly poignant
sensation in Gideon's mind. He would have told
you that it was repulsion, but it was much more
like fascinated dread.

On this night, however, he had no time for
thoughts beyond himself. He shrank from speaking even to his uncle Obed, whom he vaguely saw

standing near the door of the parish church, set
lengthwise, east and west, along the side of the
street, as he sped onward to the Market Place—a
wide oblong space, paved with cobble-stones, and
ascending on one side towards the gray arch of the
bridge across the river. After the bridge, the
houses on either side of the road meandered a little,
and very soon ceased altogether, but Gideon did
not go very far. He only crossed the bridge, and
turned aside to the towing-path beside the river.
The thought had come to him that he would walk
a little way from the bridge and wait—perhaps on
the other side of the next hawthorn hedge—for the
return of the pleasure-barge.

For a little distance the path was rough and
covered with cinders. There was Hernshaw's
brewery and its out-houses beside the river on one
side, and some coal-sheds and high windowless
buildings on the other. After these erections came
a little river-side house or two: one with a garden,
generally occupied by some Dissenting minister
or other; and one, much nearer the water's edge,
which belonged to Obed Pilcher. Gideon glanced
at this house with a sensation of relief—he was glad

that his uncle had not come home, and that he was on the other side of the river. He passed the brewery, got free of the cinders, and threw himself down on the grass of a field, on the further side of a tall hedge which effectually screened him from the eyes of townsfolk on the bridge. Here he lay and waited, until the shadows gathered thickly about him, and the moon came out above the poplar-trees.

Gradually all sounds died away. The water made a gentle plashing now and then. The scent of meadowsweet was wafted to his nostrils, and white moths fluttered dimly about him in the twilight; once an owl sailed past his head with a rush of great soft wings, otherwise he was undisturbed. Not until close upon eleven o'clock—he heard it strike from the church tower soon afterwards—was he conscious of the first faint sign of the returning water-party.

A strain of music first—the sound of voices singing. They always sang as they came home— Gideon knew that. He hated the sound, although distance made it rather sweet upon the listening air. They were singing a pretty, plaintive ditty, newer then to English ears than it is now—one of the

American plantation songs, which always have a note of melancholy beneath their quaintness. " Way down upon de Swanee River "—Gideon could himself sing it with the best of them, but he buried his fingers in his ears and would not recognise its sweetness as it drew near. Only when the boat came round a corner into the moonlight, and he could see as well as hear, did he look up. He was not quite near enough to distinguish faces, but he was sure that he could see Emmy's big white hat and the white frock and blue ribbon that she was sure to wear. He could not be mistaken in that slim white figure, even although it was encircled by the arm of a man whom Gideon vaguely knew to be Fred Chiltern.

> " All de world am sad and dreary
> Wheresoe'er I roam.
> Oh, darkies, how my heart grows weary——".

Then there was a breakdown and a laugh. The very pathos of the words, which almost brought a sob into Gideon's throat, seemed ridiculous to these young people.

" The old folks at home are welcome to see the

last of me, any time they like!" cried one reckless young voice.

"If I found the world so sad and dreary as all that, I'd go and drown myself," laughed another; and this time Gideon thrilled all over, for it was Emmy who had spoken.

"No fear," answered another, and then the boat swept on to the landing-place, and there was an indiscriminate hubbub of shouts, rattling chains, a bump or two, the sound of feet on the pathway, as the girls were jumped to land by their swains, the light laughter of voices saying good-bye. Gideon rose and looked at the little group from over the hedge. "I'll take Miss Enderby home," he heard Fred Chiltern say.

Should he interfere? For a moment he was inclined to step forward and declare his right to be Emmy Enderby's escort. Why should Chiltern see her home through the echoing streets, where the moonlight lay so white and chill upon the stones? It was *his* place—*his*, to be at Emmy's side, for had she not let him tell her that he loved her? Perhaps since then she had let Fred Chiltern tell her the same story? Gideon held back; he had forfeited his place.

In five minutes they had dispersed, and even the sound of ringing footsteps on the bridge had died away. Gideon flung himself down on the grass again, the hot tears in his eyes, the convulsive sobs in his throat. He had not cried since he was a child; but something overcame his manhood now. He wept, with his face pressed to the warm dry earth, his hands clutching restlessly at the tuft of herbage within reach. He was shaken from head to foot by the misery of a thwarted desire.

In the early light of morning he crept back to his loft over the wood-shed, and lay there until he could slip into the house unseen. No one had missed him. His movements were so erratic that even Mrs. Blake had dropped the habit of inquiring whether he were at home or not when she locked the house-door. It was known that he slept in the loft whenever he felt disposed.

Emmy Enderby was not quite happy in her mind when she awoke on Sunday morning. She had been later the night before than her mother approved, and in her own heart she knew that she had gone further in her flirtation with Fred Chiltern than she had intended to do. And she was aware that Gideon was angry—Carry Blake had left her in no doubt upon that subject—and although she told herself with a laugh that she did not care, she knew that she was a trifle afraid of his anger. She had been proud of leading in a leash the lion which no one but herself could tame; but how if the lion turned and crushed her, after all?

Emmy was very orthodox on a Sunday. She went to church in all her bravery, and sat with the quietest of her younger sisters in a pew where her new muslin and her hat with the feathers had the greatest chance of being observed by all the congregation. Then, in the afternoon, she condescended so far as to teach a class in the Sunday-school, where her services as a performer on the harmonium were also in requisition. The Sunday-school was very small and very badly managed, for the Rector was old and in delicate health, and left all such minor matters to the care of a young curate who neither knew nor cared much about the parish. It was he, however, who had asked Miss Enderby to become a teacher, and perhaps it was

partly on that account that Emmy had con-
sented.

The Enderby's shop was in the Market Place,
and not five minutes' walk from the school-house,
and at five minutes to two precisely Emmy came
out at the side-door with her bundle of little books
in her hand, feeling very pious and very well
satisfied with her own doings. She rather hoped
that she might meet Fred Chiltern on the way, and
be obliged to refuse to go for a walk with him.
"I am going to Sunday-school, Mr. Chiltern," she
imagined herself saying, with a demure droop of
her eyelids. He would wonder if she were indeed
the same girl that he had—well, talked to the night
before (a different word had been upon her lips);
and he would know that she was a good girl—a
nice girl, "and," said Emmy to herself with a
curious lack of humour, as she stepped out of the
iron-monger's house, "quite the lady." For, to
Emmy's mind, teaching in a Sunday-school brought
her up to the level of the Rectory young ladies,
who also took a class when they were at home.

She stepped out into the sunshine, her pink
starched skirts—it was the fashion of the day—

floating around her; her white leghorn hat, with its white feather, a model of daintiness. She wore a filmy white fichu, and very pale primrose kid gloves. The taste of the day was for bright colours, and Emmy knew that she looked well in them. She had bronze boots, and a lace handkerchief laden with scent, and a gold brooch and bracelets, and the youth of the neighbourhood admired her immensely. Then she was, without doubt, remarkably pretty. Her complexion was fine as the petal of a rose, and her small features were delicately cut. Her eyes were large, blue, and innocent-looking, and her curly hair was golden and abundant. It was a conventional type, but one that there could be no hesitation about—it was neither classic nor romantic nor picturesque, perhaps; it was simply very bright and very pretty. In our days, a girl with her eyes and hair would not be suffered to wear a staringly pink frock, but in the sixties pink was quite the proper thing.

She came out, radiant as the dawn, fresh as a rose, and found herself face to face with Gideon Blake, whose brow was like a thunder-cloud indeed.

4

She recoiled with a little exclamation. His face daunted her. In other ways, his appearance was better than usual; he had donned his Sunday clothes, which he sometimes disdained to wear, and had made the best of himself. But his haggard eyes and cheeks, his pale lips, his threatening gaze, as well as a certain stony determination which sat upon every feature, caused her to shrink back within the doorway, and to say rather nervously:

"Oh, Gideon, how you startled me!"

He looked at the radiant vision unappalled. He was in the mood when nothing would affect him but a simple yea or nay. Emmy's fine feathers sometimes made him a little afraid of her; but to-day he knew them for the mere externals and accessories that they were.

"I can't stay," said Emmy hurriedly. "Don't keep me, please, Gid; I am going to Sunday-school."

She made a little movement as if to pass him, but he stood blocking the way, and putting out one hand, he laid it on her wrist in a clasp that was quite gentle, yet which might tighten, as she felt, in one moment to a grip of steel.

"You are not going to Sunday-school or any-where else," he said, "until you have answered me one question."

"Oh, Gideon, don't be so silly! I shall be late. I'll go for a walk with you after school. Won't that do?"

"No, it won't do. I've been waiting too long already. I want to know whom you like best—Fred Chiltern or me?"

"Gideon, I *can't* answer a question like that all in a moment!"

"If you can't," he said, in level, unemotional tones, "you've answered it already, and I shall never ask you again. I shall never see you or speak to you again. I've made up my mind. So will you tell me in plain words, or will you not?"

"Oh, Gideon!" she cried again. Then she drew back a pace or two within the passage of the house. "I can't answer such a question out there—in the Market Place. Everyone will see. Look over there! I see Mrs. Larriper at her window opposite, laughing."

"She can't hear what we say," returned Gideon imperturbably. "I must know."

"Which I like best—Fred or you? Suppose I say Fred?"

Gideon half turned on his heel.

"Very well," he answered in a smothered voice; "then I shall know what to do."

"What will you do?" cried Emmy, half alarmed, half impatient. "There's nothing to do. What do you mean?"

"I—could—kill him!" said Gideon, between his teeth.

And he looked as if he meant it. There was a latent fierceness in his eyes and voice such as Emmy, in her peaceful English life, had never seen before. She uttered a little cry, and pulled him into the house.

"You silly boy! How can you say such dreadful things! You want to frighten me!"

"I don't want to frighten you," said Gideon doggedly. The scowl upon his forehead was more pronounced than ever; he looked fixedly at the wall, as if he did not care to meet the horror of Emmy's wide-eyed gaze. "I mean what I say. If you're going to marry Chiltern, I'd just as soon be out of the world as in it. But he should go first. If he robs me of the only thing I care for, he shall suffer for it. That would be only justice. And I give you fair warning."

" But, Gideon—Gideon," said Emmy, with face from which the rose-tints had fled, "you are mistaken. You must not talk in that way. Indeed, I—I don't like Mr. Chiltern better than you."

Gideon's eye flashed.

" You like me best?" he said, putting out both hands.

She placed hers in them—dropping her little books upon the floor—as she replied:

" Yes, yes, indeed I do!"

" Emmy—do you *love* me?"

" Oh, Gideon—yes, of course. Fancy asking me here—and now!"

They were in a narrow entry, where the odours of a past dinner were very strong, and the voices of the family could be distinctly heard through the partition-wall. Perhaps it was an odd place in which to make love. But Gideon did not care. He shut the door behind him with his foot, and took the girl's slight figure in his arms. Something in his manner—its restraint rather than its

passion—took hold of Emmy's nature and seemed
to hold it fast.   From the moment when she felt
the pressure of his lips on hers, she knew that she
belonged to him as she could belong to no one
else.   The shallow, frivolous nature was pierced
through by the shaft of his intense love and longing; she was lifted out of herself by the purest
and strongest kind of feeling that she had ever
known—by a love which seemed the fellow of Gideon's own.   But Gideon's love was of the enduring
kind ; and hers was, perhaps, a thing of rather
ephemeral growth.

He had never kissed her before; it had been
counted against him as a fault in Emmy's mind
that he had never tried to kiss her.   But now, as
his lips clung to hers, she trembled with a sensation of shame and fear, and was glad that he had
reserved his caresses for a moment of silence and
obscurity.   She was glad to hide her face upon
his shoulder, and it was her first experience of that
sort of shy reserve.

"My own love! my darling!" he murmured,
still holding her close to him.

"I must go—I really must," she panted.

"Mother or one of the children may come out at any moment."

"Yes; you can come out on the river with me."

"Oh, Gideon, not on a Sunday!"

"You went with that fellow last night; now you must come with me."

"But there is the school——"

"There's the curate to keep order. You won't go to that school any more, Emmy, so you may as well give it up at once."

Emmy felt a touch of rebellious indignation.

"Indeed, Gideon, I cannot give it up in this way——"

"Do you like the curate better than me? Then go to the school," said Gideon, suddenly releasing her hands. And Emmy felt that she had met her master; it was not to her altogether an unpleasing discovery.

"Oh no, Gideon, don't say that! I will do exactly what you like," she said humbly. "I would a great deal rather go on the river with you, only— it is Sunday, and I have on this frock; I'm afraid it will get spoiled. Let us go for a walk instead."

"Will you go on the river with me—with me *alone*—to-morrow night?" said Gideon insistently.

"Yes, I will."

"And never again without me?"

She pouted a little.

"Well, I don't know. Oh, don't be angry"—she was developing a dread of Gideon's power—"I won't go unless you allow me. Will that do, you tyrant?"

He smiled, not displeased to be called a tyrant in such sweet tones by a pair of such pretty lips, with so daintily mutinous a glance from those blue eyes. He kissed her again, and asked her to come out at once.

"My books—I have dropped them all over the place, and they are Mr. Crewe's."

"Damn Mr. Crewe!" said Gideon.

She turned a pretty, beseeching glance towards him.

"Oh, Gideon! I hope you are not going to use language like that! And you ought not to swear before a lady—without apologizing."

"I apologize, then," said he, without moving a

muscle of his face. "Only, don't stop to pick up his books, or I'll do it again."

"Am I to leave them on the floor, then?"

"I'll dispose of them," he said, giving the little volume nearest him a vicious kick. "Crewe's books indeed! There it goes—all to pieces, you see. You can't use that one again, and the other——"

"Don't touch that, it's a Prayer-book," said Emmy, with superstitious anxiety. "I should never feel happy in our engagement if you kicked a Prayer-book, Gideon. Let us come out, now, and have a nice walk."

Gideon desisted from his attack on the books, shrugged his shoulders, and followed her out of the house. The neighbours, peering through their windows, were very much amazed to see Miss Enderby turn down towards the river instead of bending her steps, as usual, to the schools.

"Ah, it's that young Blake! Poor girl! I'm sorry she's taken up with him. It'll bring her sorrow, I've no doubt—and him too, maybe."

But nothing could have been further than sorrow from the minds of Gideon and Emmy as they strolled in the meadows that afternoon, or sat in the shade of the hawthorn bushes on the river-bank. They were supremely happy—Gideon because he had attained the desire of his heart. Emmy because she was secure of her conquest. For, after those first few imperious moments, Gideon showed himself as humble a slave, as devoted a lover, as any woman could desire. Only once did the old jealous flame blaze out when he was talking to Emmy underneath the trees.

" That man—Chiltern—you did not let him make love to you, did you ? "

" I could not help his being—a little—*fond* of me, you know, Gideon," said Emmy softly.

" But you did not encourage him ? "

"Oh no, dear ! "

" Emmy—you did not ever—let him kiss you ? "

He spoke out of his knowledge of the ways of Casterby girls of Emmy's class. He was not at all surprised at the colour which burned on her cheeks as she replied—for, of course, Emmy was more sensitive, more delicate-minded, more refined, than the other girls he knew—

" Oh no, Gideon, never ! "

He believed her implicitly ; and Emmy, turning aside her flushed face, said to herself that of one thing she was certain—Gideon must never, never know !

III.

"If thou shouldst never see my face again,
Pray for my soul."

To be married in the month of November was not the choice that Emmy Enderby would naturally have made; but, as things turned out, she was not well able to help herself. Shortly after her engagement to Gideon, her father died suddenly, leaving his family quite unprovided for; and it seemed better for Emmy to marry Gideon at once than to set out on a career of her own as nursery governess or shop-girl. Gideon was young—only just twenty-one—and she was eighteen, but he was earning enough under his father to support a wife, and old Obed Pilcher's house on the river-bank was at their disposal. It was arranged, therefore, that the marriage should take place on the first of November, that Gideon should then go with his bride for a week's visit to the seaside, and return at the end of that time to Uncle Obed's house.

Everything was arranged with the most commonplace simplicity. Emmy and her mother were, in spite of their recent bereavement, in a flutter of excitement about wedding clothes. Mrs. Blake became unusually good-tempered, when the prospect of losing Gideon as a house-mate drew nearer to reality; her husband was benignly well-satisfied. Uncle Obed was in the seventh heaven of delight. All that remained was that Gideon should show himself the conventionally happy bridegroom, and this, for some reason or other, Gideon declined to do. He was not satisfactory.

For instance, on this the last evening of his bachelorhood, instead of an uproarious supper with his friends—instead, even, of hanging about the house of his beloved, and making love to her in the best parlour—he had chosen to come away from the warm, lighted rooms, to stride across the fields at the back of the Market Place, and away to the wood-yard, to his little den below the eaves.

Nobody knew that he was there. Emmy thought he had gone home, a little vexed, perhaps, because she could not give him all the attention that he desired; his own people thought that he was

with Emmy. And he was sitting gloomily in the
dark and the cold of his garret, listening to the
howl of the wind and the swish of the rain-drops
against the window-pane, looking out at the black
clouds scurrying across the heavens, and at the
twinkling of the lights in the little town, and real-
izing in a strange new way that he was beginning
another life, and that his wild-beast love of solitude
ought henceforward to have an end.

When Emmy was his wife, he would not be
free to hide himself in his den, and hack away at
pieces of wood by the hour together, or to sit and
dream of things that could never be. No doubt it
was a foolish, unmanly taste, this love of solitude
and dreaming, and it would be better for him to
give it up; but his heart sank a little within him,
nevertheless. He supposed it was because he was
"queer"; he had been called queer all his life;
even Emmy called him queer, although she loved
him. And did she love him? There, perhaps, was
the rub.

In the excitement, the almost delirious pleasure,
of the last few months, he had scarcely stopped to
ask himself the question. She had accepted him,

and sent away Fred Chiltern for his sake; surely
that was an answer. But now, when his desire was
so near fulfilment, a cold chill of doubt passed
through him. She cared about her frocks, about
her future home, about her prospects, but did she
care for *him?*

She laughed at his tastes; she could not see
anything interesting in his unconsciously artistic
woodwork. He had never dared to tell her of the
thoughts that sometimes filled his soul.

"It will be better when we are married," he
said to himself, looking out into the darkness;
"then she will begin to understand."

He was troubled sometimes by a certain unde-
fined likeness between her and his half-sister Carry,
who had always been a thorn in his side. They
had set up a giggling school-girl friendship; and
they had sometimes combined to laugh at him, and
to call him a sulky bear. The time of his betrothal
had not been all sunshine, but his eager love had
borne him through its darker moments. Now, at
the last moment, he was conscious of this odd and
(as some people would say) unnatural sinking of
heart at the coming change. Perhaps it showed

how unlike he was to others of his kind. The feeling of triumph, of elation, had left him. He was not precisely nervous, but he was afraid.

By and by he lighted a candle, and surveyed the little bare room. He had taken out of it anything that was ornamental; the carvings, the trifles that he had made for Emmy, had all gone to the new home. Some tools and pieces of wood lay about the floor; a little bench and a shelf or two were all the remaining furniture. He put out his hand and felt along the dusty shelf, for the light of the candle was very dim. Presently his hand came in contact with the objects he had been seeking: two small brown books, evidently of considerable age. He took them down, brushed the dust from their backs, and looked at them. Were they worth taking with him to Emmy's new home?

Emmy had a smart bookcase filled with brightly-bound books. Some of them were cheap standard editions of the poets, given to her as birthday presents or as prizes; others were semi-religious story-books—"Queechy," "Say and Seal," "Father Clement," and the like. Emmy had read the stories, but did not care for them; she pre-

ferred Mrs. Henry Wood and Miss Braddon. Into
the poets she had never glanced at all. Scott,
Cowper, Wordsworth, Shakespeare, Thomson's
"Seasons," and Young's "Night Thoughts"—what
were they to her? But she liked the bindings,
scarlet, or blue, or green, with a good deal of
gilding on the backs; and she was quite proud
of her library. Gideon also was not much of a
reader, and knew what was inside those bindings
rather less than herself. He did not think that
his two poor little shabby books would look well
on the shelves beside Emmy's grand volumes, yet
he did not like to throw them away. He had
another store of his own—a few boys' books, a
few that treated of popular science; these were to
fill a shelf in a back room of his new house, but
he had a reluctance to let these two go amongst
them. Emmy would finger them, and call them
rubbish; and he would not be able to tell her
why he valued them. He knew too well that
singular incapacity for speech which was beginning to attack him whenever he felt most deeply.

He had never read either of these books. He
cared for them from the instinct of old habit.

His grandmother had given one of them to him long ago, and told him its history. It was a relic of ancient days—a book of Latin prayers, totally unintelligible to her, and to Gideon as well; but there was just the ghost of a story attached to it. In brown and faded ink upon the flyleaf was written the name of "John Gideon Blake." Below it there was a date, "November 1st, 1584," and a few words which ignorant Gideon could not make out, but which his grandmother had told him signified, "Pray for my soul." A Popish relic, as his grandmother had said; and the John Gideon Blake to whom it had belonged was of course no ancestor of theirs, but only a collateral— a good thing, considering that he had been a Romish priest, beheaded for treason in the reign of Good Queen Bess. The date in the book was that of his death, written with his own hand before he went to execution, as well as the words which Gideon could not read: "Ora pro animâ meâ." Nothing more was known of him, and the book had survived, as if by miracle, to the present day, having been carefully kept, it was said, by the priest's brother, who had transmitted it to his Protestant descendants. Thus it came into the hands of Gideon, who had indignantly demanded (in his early years) why *he* should have been called after a Popish priest?

"There was always a Gideon among the Blakes," his grandmother had told him. "Your grandfather—he was Gideon, too. That's why I give the book to you. They say it's valuable; it might fetch money if ever you wanted to sell it."

Gideon took the book and kept it. Nothing on earth would have induced him to part with it again; in spite of his dislike to "Papists," which he had caught from Obed Pilcher and other relations, there was some sort of distinction in having had a great-uncle, ever so many generations back, who was important enough to be put to death for treason. Gideon had rather a sympathy with anyone who rebelled against the powers that be.

No, he would not take this book with him to his new home. He would let it lie on the shelf. It would be safe there; nobody came to that room save himself.

The other book was one of a very different
school.   It was " The Pilgrim's Progress," and it
had belonged to his mother.   Gideon had never
troubled to read it, but as it had been his mother's
book, he did not like to throw it away.   He
turned over the leaves musingly, then looked once
more at the flyleaf of the Latin book, which was,
in fact, an ancient breviary.   The date . caught
his eye, " November the second "—why, that would
be his own wedding-day.   He would be married
on the very day when this kinsman of his went
to his death.   Gideon caught his breath a little.
It flashed across his mind that if he had remembered, he would not have chosen the second of
November for his wedding-day.

He was too ignorant to know anything about
Old Style and New Style, and the difference of
the calendar, neither had he any religious asso-
ciation connected with the day.   He was a provincial English lad, and All Souls' Day was quite
unknown to him.   But there was something that
moved him in the thought of this man, of his own
blood, who had been executed on the very day
(as Gideon thought) which was to bring happi-

ness to Emmy and himself. And he had wanted people to pray for his soul! A Popish superstition, for what was the good of praying for the soul of one who was dead and buried?—but perhaps that was his way of asking to be remembered. Gideon slipped the book into his pocket, instead of putting it back in its place, and said "Poor chap!" to himself, with a thrill of involuntary pity. To go out of the world like that, nearly three hundred years ago, and to be quite forgotten, while he, Gideon, was alive and young and about to marry Emmy Enderby!

He blew out his candle, and stood staring out of the window for some time, troubled against his will, as if something—somebody—had called to him out of that past of which he knew so little. A more imaginative person than Gideon Blake might have fancied that the dead priest's spirit had come back to earth to whisper in his ear. That was what would have been said in mediæval times. But Gideon was the creature of his circumstances, and he lived in a *milieu* which forbade morbid imaginings of the sort. A prosaic artisan, in a prosaic country town, knowing nothing of religion save from the strongly Protestant point of view, and utterly intolerant of superstition—how should any such foolish notion present itself even to his untutored mind? It would be more natural to this generation to suggest that even in this commonplace Lincolnshire family there might be a *sport*—a freak of Nature—a "throw-back," by which the modern young carpenter reproduced in a different environment the nature, the instincts, the tendencies of a fanatical Roman priest who died for his cause three hundred years ago.

He turned abruptly from the window at last, and left the room without making any further researches. He went out into the muddy, unlighted lane, and made his way, despite wind and rain, into the main street of the town. With hands thrust in his pockets, and head down-bent, he looked extremely unlike a bridegroom, and Emmy would not have been flattered if she had seen him pacing the wet street in this guise. Fortunately for him, he met none of his acquaintances; the rain poured too heavily for any of them to be abroad, and the pavements were deserted.

A flood of light on the wet flags before him

attracted his attention. He looked up and started a little at finding himself just before the iron gates that led to the Roman Catholic chapel, which had a small green space between its doors and the road. The doors were open, and one or two people were putting up their umbrellas and coming towards the gate. Gideon hesitated. It seemed to him a curious coincidence that he should be standing at this gate so soon after looking at the book once used by the one Romanist (so far as he knew) in his family. There was no coincidence, of course, about the matter, for he passed close by that gate every day of his life, but he had never before felt inclined to enter it. Some curiosity stirred him; he wondered, for the first time, what these ignorant Papists believed; he wondered whether anyone in that little chapel could explain to him why John Gideon Blake, priest, had desired his friends to pray for his soul. He went inside the gates.

He was not likely to get much for his pains. It was between eight and nine o'clock, and the congregation was dispersing after an eloquent and impassioned sermon from a stranger upon the blessedness of the saints. Gideon knew nothing

about saints, and would only have stared if anyone
had told him that it was All Saints' Day. He
went into the church and gazed blankly at the
empty seats, at the wealth of white flowers on the
altar, at the rows of candles which someone was
putting out with an extinguisher at the end of a
stick. A great wooden crucifix brought from Nu-
remberg, life-size and coloured, startled him more
than he would have liked to say. He had never
seen such a thing before. He looked round,
caught a woman's eyes fixed on him in wonder,
and retreated in guilty confusion to the vestibule.
Here for a moment he waited, for the rain was
coming down in torrents. He thought himself
a fool for having come out at all.

"Can I do anything for you?" said a voice
at his ear.

He turned hastily, and found that the woman
whom he had seen looking at him, had followed
him out of the church. Woman? She was not
a woman, she was a girl only, and he knew her
face. She was one of the Lisle family at Casterby
Park; they were all Roman Catholics, he knew.
There were two or three girls; this one was the

eldest, but she was always spoken of as "Miss Frances," because she had an aunt living at the Park who was Miss Lisle.

· "I mean," the sweet clear voice went on, "did you want anything? did you want anybody in particular?"

"No," said Gideon. He felt that his answer was abrupt and harsh, but he did not know what to say. He wished desperately that he had never come.

"I am waiting for my uncle—Father O'Brien is my uncle," said the young lady, alluding, as Gideon knew, to the priest who served the little chapel at Casterby. "He is going to drive home with me. I thought you might perhaps be looking about for him."

Did she think him a possible convert? Gideon scowled at her as the thought crossed his mind. And yet she did not look as if she had any ulterior motive for her question. There was something in her face that pleased him, although he could not have told you why.

Frances Lisle was nineteen years of age. She was rather under than over the middle height,

and she had never been considered beautiful. But
there was a peculiar serenity on the broad in-
telligent brows, and in the soft gray eyes, which
made her face pleasant to look upon. Her rip-
pling brown hair was fastened into a soft knot
behind her head, very unlike the hard glossy
lump called a chignon in these days. Her face
had very little colour, and the sensitive curves
of her lips were none the less beautiful because
they were, in a sense, contradicted by the square-
ness of her white chin. She had the look of a
supremely reasonable woman, of a woman whose
gentleness comes from sympathy, comprehension,
intelligence, not from weak compliance. It depended a little upon your own nature whether
you were more struck by the sweetness or the
strength of her face. Gideon saw the strength.

"I came in out of curiosity," he said, almost
sullenly. "I saw the doors open, and I wondered what was going on."

"Oh yes, I see. It is All Saints' Day, and
we have had Benediction and a sermon," said
Frances, simply. "You are not—a Catholic?"

Gideon shook his head vehemently.

"Oh dear no! But"—faltering a little—"I suppose I had a relation once who was. His name is in this book," he said, producing the little brown volume from his pocket. He had immediately afterwards a sensation of shame at the thought that he could show to this stranger a book which he had kept carefully from Emmy's eyes. "I was told by my grandmother that he was a priest, and I wanted to know what sort of a book it was. I think that was partly my idea in coming in here; I thought that Mr. O'Brien would tell me, perhaps."

He purposely abstained from saying Father O'Brien, although the good old priest was usually known by that title; but Frances did not notice the omission. She made a little exclamation when her eyes fell on the fly-leaf of the book.

"Oh!" she said, colouring—Gideon could not imagine why; but it was from pure surprise and pleasure—"this is very interesting! He was a relation of yours, was he? This is a breviary —a service-book, used by our priests, you know. What an old book!"

She looked up at him questioningly. Gideon

gave the information that he felt she wanted from him, though with a curious reluctance.

"He was a brother of my great-great—more great than I can count—great-grandfather, and he was beheaded for treason in Queen Elizabeth's time," he said doggedly. He could not at all understand the flash of emotion that passed across the young lady's face.

"He was a martyr, then? He died for his faith? How splendid for you to have such an example before you! But I forgot—you are not of our religion. Oh, what a pity!"

Gideon held out his hand for the book.

"I'm no Papist, certainly," he said. "If he was executed for treason, I dare say it served him right. I felt a little curious about the book; that's why I asked what it was. I don't know Latin myself."

"But it is a relic—a real relic," said Frances, over whose eyes a sudden cloud of pity had stolen. She was what the world calls a bigot—a *dévote* in her way—having been educated in a convent, and taught to look upon England as a heathen, unregenerate land. She could not help feeling as if this

young man were a savage, into whose ignorant
hands some very precious thing had fallen, of which
he could not possibly estimate the value and advantage. She was sorry to give him back the book.
"I wish you would let my uncle see it; he would
be very much interested. We should value it very
much if you thought of parting with it——"

"Parting with it!" cried Gideon, almost angrily. "I should never think of such a thing.
Why, it's been in the family for three hundred
years. I only wanted to know what the book was
about."

" Would you like some of it to be translated and
explained to you ? " said Frances quickly.

"No, thank you. It's only prayers and services, you say—I don't want them. I thought it
might be something different. It isn't the book I
care so much about as the—the name—and all
that."

"Yes, the name and the inscription," said Miss
Lisle. "'Pray for my soul.' You don't do that,
do you, as you are a Protestant ? But—may I
look again ? Why, to-morrow is the date of his
death."

"And my wedding-day," said Gideon, with an odd smile.

"Is it really? Yes, I remember hearing of it. Your father comes to the Park sometimes, I think," said Frances, dropping her eyes. She had only just made out his identity, and she was a little sorry that he was the black sheep of whom she had sometimes heard. But she was not sorry that she had spoken to him. In spite of her simplicity, she knew quite well that she was one of the great ladies of the place, and that it was quite within her right to speak to whomsoever she pleased in Casterby. The Blakes were her father's tenants, and Joseph Blake was a respectable person and a clever workman: she knew that. "All Souls' Day seems to us a strange day for a marriage," she went on, with a little smile, "because it is on that day that we pray for our dead. I will have a Mass said for this martyred priest, your great-uncle, Mr. Blake, on the second of November every year. He shall not be forgotten any more, although his own people do not pray for his soul."

Gideon turned a startled, incredulous eye upon her.

"Pray? What's the good of praying?" he said, almost rudely. Then he took the book out of her hand and put it back into his pocket. "I suppose I ought to thank you—in his name—but I can't see the good of it."

"I shall pray for you, too, then," said Frances, her gray eyes shimmering through a mist of tears. "Perhaps you will be glad of it some day. Here is my uncle. May I introduce you to him, and show him the book?"

"No, no—I'd rather not," said Gideon, hurriedly. He was utterly confused and astonished by her words, and did not know the extent of his own discourtesy. "I'm very much obliged to you, but I must go."

"Good-bye, then," said Frances, extending a small ungloved hand. "I shall think of you to-morrow. I hope you will be happy. And I will not forget to pray for your uncle's soul."

"Why, what good will it do him?" said Gideon, as he awkwardly shook her hand and turned away.

He plunged into the darkness, regardless of the rain, only anxious to escape from Frances's gentle enthusiasm, and from the peering inquisition of the

sacristan, who was hovering in the background, and
the keen, kindly eyes of Father O'Brien, who came
hurriedly down the aisle in search of his niece.
The carriage from the Park was waiting at the
gate; its red lamps shone through the misty gloom,
and the horses, invisible from the chapel-door,
pawed the ground and made the harness jingle in
an impatience which the coachman shared. Father
O'Brien handed his niece into the carriage, and
they drove away.

"And who was that young fellow you were
talking with, Frances?" asked the uncle during
that homeward drive.

Frances told the story, ending with some lamen-
tation over the fate of the book in Gideon's
keeping.

"The lad has a right to it," said the priest good-
humouredly. "And it may be the means of his
conversion in the long-run."

"Ah, yes!" said Frances eagerly. "I hardly
thought of that. There have been cases, have there
not, where the possession of a precious relic——"
She stopped short, scarcely knowing why. "At
any rate, we can pray for him," she added in a lower

tone, "that he may some day become a member of the one true Church."

It may be as well to say here, once and for all, that Frances Lisle's hopes were never realized. Gideon Blake was not converted to Roman Catholicism at any period of his life. His creed, such as it was, was fashioned on very different lines; but the important thing in this interview between himself and Frances was the formation of a subtle bond of sympathy which outlived all divergencies of creed.

While Frances and her uncle were swiftly and luxuriously conveyed to their abode, Gideon, with a strange sense of tingling confusion, made his way through the darkness to Obed Pilcher's little house beside the river. There was a side road or lane off the Market Place, which brought him to its door. It was badly lighted, but it was better than the other ways of approach—the river path on the one side, or the fields upon the other. In summer the situation was delightful: the gleaming river just outside the garden palings, the fragrant meadows stretching away into the distance, the town so near, and yet almost out of sight. But in winter! For

6

the first time Gideon had a doubt. The fields were
full of mist, and he could hear the river lapping up
to the very palings of his garden. He remembered
that he had seen the meadows under water many a
time, and he wondered, a little humorously,
whether Emmy would dislike the darkness and the
damp.

He had almost to feel his way up the garden-
path to the green door. The house was little more
than a cottage, but a pretty cottage, with creeping
plants growing over the brickwork, and a little
porch in front. The garden was full of sweetest
old-fashioned flowers in the summer-time, and
shaded by tall poplars and a great beech-tree. But
now the wind whistled in the bare branches, and
the garden-beds were desolate. Gideon shivered as
he pushed open the door.

Obed Pilcher came out to meet him. He had
been sitting in the kitchen with his pipe. The
front parlour had been refurnished for Emmy's use,
and he would not desecrate it with smoke. His
weather-beaten face beamed with smiles when he
saw Gideon, but the smiles were succeeded by a
look of anxiety.

"Why, Gideon," he said, "thou'rt wet through, lad! Thee shouldn't be out when it siles down o' rain like this—on th' neet afore th' wedding, too!"

"I'm all right," said Gideon, shaking himself like a big dog. "I'll sit by the fire a bit, and take a drop of whisky if you've any to give me, and I shall be all right."

"Come on, then," said Obed.

He led the way into the clean, red-bricked, yellow-walled kitchen, and stirred up the fire, until its flames were reflected in every brightly-burnished tin or plate that stood upon the dresser shelves. Gideon took off his coat and boots, and sat down to dry himself in silence. Obed mixed him a stiff glass of hot whisky-and-water, with the view of warming and cheering the intending bridegroom. But he wondered a little when he saw Gideon toss it off; he had not often seen "the lad" touch anything stronger than water. It suddenly crossed the old man's mind that it would be a terrible thing if Gideon, with his fierce temper and great physical strength, should at any time "take to drink."

Some time elapsed before the young man spoke.

He roused himself to glance round the kitchen and to say, rather hesitatingly :

" Will she like it, do you think ? "

" Emmy ? She'll be a fool if she don't ! " said Uncle Obed.

" I'd like to look at the parlour again," said Gideon.

He took up a candle, and went in his stockinged feet down the little passage to the sitting-room, with old Obed after him. Both men religiously left their pipes behind.

The sitting-room was furnished according to the dictates of Casterby taste at that time. It had a Kidderminster carpet, with red and white flowers on a green ground, a " suite " of furniture of walnut and green damask, green curtains to match, and stiff lace ones inside them, partially concealing the new Venetian blinds. There was a gilt-framed mirror over the marble mantelpiece, and some oleographs on the walls. Emmy's smart bookcase and cottage piano also helped to fill the room, and white anti-macassars abounded in legion. It was a stiff, inartistic, glaring little room, with its white and gold wall-paper, and its ornaments of green glass vases, with gilt snakes round their stems; but to Gideon, who knew no better, it was like a shrine.

"It's a real lady's room," said Obed admiringly.

"Ay, but it's not near good enough for her," Gideon replied. He walked round the room, touching a cushion here, an antimacassar there, with a caressing hand. "It's as much as I can do," he said in a low tone; "but when I get on in the world, Uncle Obed, I'll make a palace for her. I'd like a house like the Squire's, with all those paintings and carvings that I've seen in the hall when I went with father; they're much prettier, of course, than anything I could get for Emmy, but I suppose they cost a lot of money. I should like her to have everything of the best."

"Eh, lad, you'll get all you want in time," said his uncle.

"Well, I hope so, if I work hard. I mean to work hard—for her sake; and yours too, Uncle Obed. But for you, I mightn't have a home to give her—a nest for the bird. We shall be very happy here, Emmy and I."

There was a wistful tone in his voice. It was almost as though he were answering some objection advanced by another voice—disposing of scruples, as if he were called upon to defend himself. Obed grunted, and made no other answer; he did not understand the mood.

"I'm going to turn over a new leaf when I'm married," said Gideon, pacing about the room. "I've thought it over a good many times. I told Emmy so—at least, I tried to tell her. She knows so little of the world that, of course, she could not exactly understand; but she will be glad to think of it by and by. I think I'll go to church on Sunday mornings, Uncle Obed, and sit with Emmy. It's all very well to loaf about in the fields of a Sunday, smoking and enjoying one's self; but it isn't quite the thing for a married man, is it? And, besides, after a time there may be——. Well, anyhow, I shall be a different man when Emmy's here."

"Lord bless thee, lad!" said the old man, "I doan't knaw about Emmy; but I haven't much fear for thee."

IV.

"You shall not go," said Gideon.

"I shall go if I like," Emmy cried out angrily.

There was a pause. Husband and wife faced each other with an ugly look in their eyes. Emmy was scarlet with wrath; but Gideon was deadly white.

He spoke at last, in a low but distinct tone.

"I'm your husband—and your master. I forbid you to go."

She laughed mockingly.

"I should like to know how you can prevent me. I shall do just as I choose. Master indeed! Do you think I am going to be a slave? But it is just what I might have expected. Everybody warned me against your awful, abominable temper. Everybody told me that I had a very small chance of happiness. And I have had none at all. You

83

have made me miserable—*miserable;* and I wish I had never married you!"

"You needn't say that in front of the boy," said Gideon with some difficulty. But Emmy was not to be stayed.

"Oh, indeed! The boy is to be considered before me, is he? I only wish he were old enough to understand what a tyrant his father is. Perhaps, when he is grown up, I shall have somebody to defend me——"

"You don't need defence—your tongue's enough. Do as you please; but you shall not take the boy with you. John, come here."

Gideon held out his hand to a little fellow of three years old, who stood against the wall with stiff white petticoats outspread, and hands behind his back, a puzzled, uncomprehending spectator of the scene. Some instinct of affection for his old dream had made the father name his child John Gideon, after the long-dead owner of the breviary. Emmy had been very angry about the name. The baby had been baptized in a hurry while the mother was ill, and she had meant him to be named Reginald Arthur. She now called the boy Johnny or Jacky; but Gideon seldom called him anything but John, which seemed somewhat solemn and inapplicable to the fair little fellow, with dark eyes and curls of gold, sturdy and chubby as he was.

"Come here, John," Gideon repeated, and the boy ran towards him and hid his face against his father's knee. He was a sensitive child, and quivered all over when he heard his mother's passionate voice.

"It's always the same! You always interfere between me and any little pleasure I may be going to have. Why shouldn't I go out on the river? Why shouldn't I take Jacky? If *you* are so dull and stupid as not to want any amusement yourself, you need not prevent me from having any."

Her voice was shrill, her face red from excitement; her hair was loosened and hung half down her back. Gideon looked at her unemotionally, and wondered for a moment where her prettiness had gone. Her skin had lost its delicacy, and her dress was untidy. She hardly looked like the Emmy Enderby who had won Gideon's heart.

As for him, he was less altered than his wife,

and the alteration was, in some respects, for the
better. He was still spare and sinewy; but his
shoulders had broadened, and his frame filled out,
and his aspect was that of a more prosperous man
than in days of old. His shock of black hair still
made his face look heavy, and his brows were bent
in a perpetual frown; but his features and expression had gained definiteness, and there was less sullen gloom in his bearing than in his boyhood. But
the added brightness in his life did not come from
Emmy—only from Emmy's child.

The cause of dispute was simple. In the four
and a half years that had elapsed since Gideon's
marriage, the Saturday evening excursions down
the river in Mortlock's barge had fallen greatly into
disrepute. Cases of drunkenness were never rare,
and some serious scandals owed their origin to these
Saturday merry-makings. Casterby was not strict
in its views; but it rose up and drew the line some-
where, now and then, and it had decreed that Mortlock's barge, at a shilling a head, was not respectable. But Mrs. Gideon Blake greatly resented this
deprivation of her privileges, and had announced
her intention of going to the Three Bridges (the

name of a very popular old inn at some distance down the river), with some of her friends, on the first Saturday in July. Mr. Fred Chiltern, with his "young lady"; Carry Blake, now seventeen and the biggest flirt in Casterby; and several other young people, were to be of the party—to which, moreover, Emmy had determined to take her little boy. And then Gideon had put down his foot, and declared that she should not go.

It was Saturday afternoon when he first realized what his wife intended to do. And he had stubbornly and imperiously ordered her to take off her finery and remain at home. The boat was timed to start at five, and Gideon's interference took place at four o'clock, an hour late enough to give his wife some cause for vexation. She was just on the point of beginning to dress for the jaunt when he interfered.

"John shall not go," said the father, putting his hand on the boy's head. "If for no other reason, the weather's damp, and the boy's chest is weak, and he's not fit to be kept up till eleven o'clock. I won't have it. Do as you like yourself, but you shall not take John."

"I know that you are fonder of John than you are of me," said Emmy spitefully.

Gideon's dark eyes glowed; he raised them to her face with a strange expression, but lowered them almost immediately.

"Am I?" he said.

"Yes, you are, and you know it. Perhaps you'd like me to leave you altogether, and then you and Jacky and Uncle Obed could have the place to yourselves. You'd like that, wouldn't you?"

If Gideon's eyes had glowed before, they blazed now. He put John away from him, and took a step towards his wife, with livid face and threatening hand. He had no intention of striking her, but he scarcely knew what he did.

"Leave me?" he said. "*Leave* me?"

He said nothing more, but he seized her by the shoulder, and Emmy cowered and shrieked under the iron grip of his strong hand.

"Gideon, don't! You hurt me!"

"Hurt you!" he exclaimed violently. "Do you never hurt *me?*"

The force of his hand shook her slight form, and although he had no intention of injuring her,

the very suddenness with which he removed his
grasp sent her backward against the wall breath-
less and sobbing with fear. He walked straight out
of the room and out of the house, almost beside
himself with pain and passion, little heeding the
hysterical cry which his wife sent after him—a cry
that declared herself all the more determined to
have her own way. He was blind and deaf with
anger, and with something else which was not
anger, but bitterness and regret and sickening disappointment. He loved Emmy still, but it had
become very plain to him of late that she cared
little about him.

He did not stop to consider whether or not she
would obey him. He supposed that she would go
her own way, leaving the child in the care of the
maid servant. Uncle Obed would be in presently,
and he was always glad to look after little John.
Gideon turned into the fields, where, by a footpath,
he could make his way to the wood-yard in Dane
Street, and betook himself to the loft where he had
spent so many idle hours in days gone by.

It was still his place of refuge in moments
when he wanted to be alone. He flung himself

down on the bench before the window, and rested
his chin in his hands. He did not look at the
glowing landscape, or fall into his old habit of
dreams. He had lost the tendency to that side
of life. His mind was absorbed by the consideration of things as they were now.

For some months his marriage had seemed
perfectly satisfactory. Emmy had grumbled more
or less at the quietness of her life, at the damp-
ness of the house, at the smallness of her husband's income, but the complaints had not meant
unhappiness. Emmy was one of the women who
always grumbled. She felt herself personally
injured if anyone in her own class of life had
a finer house, a more expensive gown than herself; it seemed to her that Providence was
treating her shabbily. The best things, as far
as she knew them, were hers by right, and when
they were not showered into her lap, somebody
—it might be the Governor of the world, or it
might be only her husband, but *somebody*—was
to blame. When she married, her views of what
was due to her were limited by ignorance. Unfortunately, every month and every year increased

her knowledge of the various pleasures and lux-
uries attainable in this world, and her opportu-
nities of achieving them—not to speak of her
husband's income—did not increase in a like
ratio.

At first Gideon took no notice. He was not
by nature inclined to notice small things, and
his wife's complaints were mere pin-pricks. After
John's birth, however, they became more shrill
and insistent, and he began to be vaguely annoyed by them. But there was no serious quarrel
until he discovered that her fondness for dress
had involved her deeply in debt, and that he
was responsible for far more than he knew how
to pay. Then he spoke angrily, and drove his
wife into a hysterical fit of weeping, which
frightened him and made him for the moment
amenable to her slightest wish. But when there
came to be no novelty about her hysterical fits,
and when the debts, and the wants, and the ill-
temper went on increasing, then Gideon came
to the point of wondering whether his marriage
was a happy one or not. *Now* there was no
doubt about the matter; Emmy had avowed

herself unhappy, and he was sounding the depths of a misery such as he had never known before.

Throughout it all, he loved her. Even when she complained and grumbled and fretted, his thoughts were tender towards her. He was not the man to give love once and take it back again. Such changes of mind belong to men of shallower nature than Gideon Blake's. It never seemed really possible for him to change.

Nevertheless, as he had a somewhat violent and sullen temper, and was not accustomed to self-control, he very often behaved roughly and harshly towards her, and alienated her volatile affections from him by a manner which effectually masked the true feeling of his heart. A less frivolous woman might have understood him better; but Emmy was convinced by this time that he did not care for her, that he was "a bear" and "a brute," and she seemed to delight in opposing his wishes and irritating his temper. He had no longer any illusions on the subject; he believed her dislike of him to be even more deeply rooted than it was. For it would have been hard for him to realize, well as he knew her, that a few judiciously-chosen presents—a silk dress or two, a gold chain, a pretty bracelet—would have restored to him all the love of which her heart was capable.

In the quiet of his lonely rooms he almost wished that he had never married. He remembered the days when he could at least come and go at will, could shut himself away from stinging speeches and undeserved reproaches, could brood for hours over his own thoughts and shape strange figures out of carven wood at the same time, absorbed partly in his dreams and partly in the dear delight of creation. The instinct of the anchorite, the solitary, was strong in him. Rather than be tied for life to an uncongenial mate, he said to himself that he would sooner always be alone.

But then, there was the child! Compensation came in there. If he were alone in the world, he would not be the father of that round-faced fair-haired creature, with the fearless eyes and stubborn chin, so like yet so unlike his own. That fair, round, self-willed little lad belonged to him in heart and soul, if Emmy did not.

7

Gideon worshipped him, without measuring the strength of his love. The world was not a wilderness while Johnny was in existence. There was always somebody to look for Gideon's coming—somebody to whom the sound of his step brought joy. Marriage was not entirely a failure, since it had put baby John into his arms.

Vaguely comforted at last, he rose up to go to his home. After all, Uncle Obed and John would be there. Emmy would have gone to her noisy, disreputable picnic, and would not be back till late in the evening. It did not occur to Gideon that he might have gone with her. Such companionship of husband and wife was not customary; and his detestation of the persons whom she called friends was too complete to be concealed. He could not possibly have gone with her, and simulated ordinary politeness.

Silence and loneliness had restored his composure. As he walked with long strides across the fields, he reflected that Emmy would be out, and that he and John and Uncle Obed would have tea by themselves. He took the trouble to turn into the main street and buy some "goodies" for

John. They would sit on the bench in the garden after tea, and John should not go to bed till ten. In this unauthorized way he would find consolation for Emmy's absence, for Emmy's ill-temper, for Emmy's want of love.

But when he neared his own house, he was struck by something unusual in its appearance, some sort of stir and excitement on the river-bank. Two or three persons were hanging over the palings, a small boat was moored to the little landing-stage just outside the garden, the front-door stood wide open, and there were strange trails of water on the garden-path and the stone flags at the door. And surely two or three people were standing in the passage. Was one of them the doctor? A qualm of fear passed through Gideon's mind as he quickened his steps in drawing near. He hardly knew how he got through the gate or arrived at last at the door, where his strained eyes and paling face put the question which his lips refused to ask.

"Don't be alarmed, he is quite safe," were the first words he heard. Who said them? He knew the sweet, clear voice, but there was a mist before his eyes. It was Frances Lisle who laid her hand upon his arm.

" Your little boy met with an accident; he fell into the water, Mr. Blake; but he was pulled out almost immediately, and I think he will be none the worse for it."

" Where is he? where is he?" stammered Gideon, with wild eyes.

" He is in bed, and his mother is upstairs with him," said Frances soothingly. " Here is the doctor; you can ask him for yourself."

Why was *she* here? Even at that moment a flash of wonder passed through Gideon's brain. But he had not time to ask the question. He would have made an immediate rush to the stairs, had not the way been blocked by the doctor—a burly figure, filling up the width of the little passage and putting out a firm white hand to arrest the young man's steps.

" Come, Gideon, you needn't worry yourself. The little lad's in bed and only needs to be kept quiet. His mother is with him: I've told her to stay until he is asleep."

" He'll go to sleep quicker with me than

with her; he always does," said Gideon
sharply.

"Nonsense! You are not to go up: do you
hear?"

"He is hurt—and you won't tell me, is that
it?" asked the young man, in a tone which, though
low, was so fierce that Frances involuntarily
started.

"Nothing of the kind, don't be a fool!" said
the doctor, who had known Gideon all his life
and could afford to be peremptory with him; "it
is only that the child has had a ducking and I
want him to get to sleep as quickly and as quietly
as possible, otherwise he may have a touch of fever.
Now, mind, I forbid more than one person in his
room for the present."

"Then you may get Emmy away," said Gideon
doggedly; "for I shall sit by the child."

The doctor elevated his eyebrows and glanced
at Miss Lisle, as if to call her to his assistance;
and Frances, thus appealed to, threw herself into
the breach.

"I want very much to tell you how it happened, Mr. Blake," she said, "if you can spare

me a minute or two before you go upstairs. I saw the accident myself, and it was a friend of mine—a gentleman who is visiting us just now—who took him out of the water."

" Yes, come in and hear all about it," said the doctor genially, pushing Gideon before him towards the door of the little parlour. " What are you thinking of, Gideon, not to ask Miss Lisle to sit down? The gentleman—Captain Hamilton, is it not?—is upstairs, changing his clothes for some of yours, I believe. Obed is looking after him."

In some confusion, Gideon pushed open the door of the sitting-room, and Frances entered it, not without curiosity to see what the sitting-room of this strange, dark-eyed young man and his pretty wife was like. She was disappointed if she expected to find any trace of superior tastes. or aspirations. The green damask and the flowery carpet were horrible in her eyes; the gilt looking-glass and the oleographs were abominations. And worse than all was the appearance of the girl, who rose in some embarrassment from the couch when Frances entered; for she was even more vulgar-looking than the room, and yet she was introduced by the doctor as " my friend Gideon's sister, Miss Carry Blake."

Frances, whose tastes, although simple, were extremely refined, was for a moment revolted by the aspect of the room and of the girl; then her kindlier instincts came into play. It was not, perhaps, Gideon's fault, it was the fault of his friends, of his wife, probably, that the room was hideous. And she could not help liking him for the anxiety which he displayed about his boy. She gave her little account of the disaster, looking straight at him so as to avoid the sight of the antimacassars and oleographs, and of Carry, with her earrings and her feathers, on the sofa.

" I was on the river in a small boat with my brother and Captain Hamilton," she said. " We were quite at the side, among some rushes, when we saw a big boat—a sort of barge—coming up——"

" Mortlock's barge," said the doctor, with a nod. Gideon set his teeth.

" We waited, so as to be out of the way of the

wash while they went by," continued Frances. " Everyone seemed to be very merry on board, and just when they passed us, I noticed a little boy clambering about—I think he was trying to see how far he could lean over the side. I called out—for nobody seemed to be looking after him—and at that moment he overbalanced himself and fell into the water."

" I'm sure," said Miss Carry volubly from the sofa, " we had only turned our heads away just for a minute; we had been looking after him as carefully as possible, Gideon, both Emmy and me, and if we had told him once to come away from the side, we had told him a dozen times; but Jacky was always a naughty boy——"

She was suddenly met by such a black look from Gideon that she was awed into silence.

" Who took him out of the water?" said her brother, in a half-stifled voice.

Miss Lisle was observed to colour as she replied:

" Captain Hamilton jumped into the water directly, and my brother rowed to the place and took him into the boat. Then we found out to whom he belonged, and brought him home, and Mrs. Blake and some of her friends came back too."

"Your uncle was here," said Dr. Miller, in his hearty voice, "and he knew exactly what to do—had the boy in a hot bath in no time, and in bed with hot blankets. There was scarcely any need for me, but Mr. Gerald Lisle was so kind as to fetch me, and I'm glad, Gideon, that I can't be of any use—ha, ha!"

The doctor's genial laugh dispelled the gloom which seemed to have settled on the party. Gideon said something about his gratitude to Captain Hamilton, and asked if he should go upstairs and see that his guest had all he required But footsteps were at that moment heard on the stairs, and Obed Pilcher appeared, ushering Captain Hamilton into the room.

Gideon was usually slow of speech, but gratitude was warm at his heart just then, and made it easy for him to utter a few words of thanks. Miss Lisle's friend received them with offhand good-humour, as if he were in the habit of saving lives every day and thought nothing of the occurrence. He had found a suit of Gideon's flannels to fit him tolerably well, for he was a tall man, though of slighter build than Blake's. His age was thirty-five, but he looked at least five years older; the crow's feet were thick round his eyes, and his hair was growing a little thin at the temples. He had a long nose, and a fair moustache; in fact, he was not unlike the conventional hero of the novels in which Emmy Blake loved to revel; and Carry, who had adopted many of her sister-in-law's tastes, eyed him with open admiration.

Young Gerald Lisle had, it seemed, gone for the carriage, which had been put up in Casterby while he and his sister took Captain Hamilton for a row on the river, and Frances was to wait until it came for her. There was a minute or two of awkwardness: Gideon had nothing to say for himself, and Carry, although not particularly shy, was too busily engaged in studying Miss Lisle's dress to have any time for conversation.

She decided in her own mind that Miss Lisle was very badly dressed. Everyone knew that she had money, and persons with money ought to dress according to their position. She did not know exactly how she would have liked Miss Lisle to dress, but she was quite sure that simple brown holland was inappropriate, and so were the brown straw hat and brown ribbons and gauntleted yellow gloves. To say that this costume was excellently adapted for boating would not have satisfied Carry's mind at all. Nor did it occur to her that Miss Lisle was going home to dress for dinner. In Carry Blake's station people dressed for tea. She supposed that Miss Lisle would wear that brown holland all the evening, and in her eyes this was almost worse than a crime. She concluded in her own mind, with a contemptuous sniff, that Miss Lisle dressed in that funny way because she was a Roman Catholic, though the connection between brown holland and a religious faith might not be apparent at first sight.

While the awkward pause still lasted, there came a rush as of flying skirts along the passage; the door was opened hastily, and Mrs. Blake appeared.

"He's asleep, doctor—fast asleep," she said breathlessly, "and Kezia's sitting with him; but I felt I *must* come down just to say my thanks to the gentleman who rescued my child—my darling little

Jacky! Oh, what should I have done if he had been drowned!"

She had never looked prettier. The excitement of the afternoon had only brought a rose-flush to her cheeks; her eyes swam with tears, but the eyelids were not reddened, and her rosy lips were parted in the most appealing of curves. Her golden hair stood up in natural waves and curls like an aureole round her fair brow, and with her slender hands outstretched, and her graceful form bent slightly forward in her impulsive burst of gratitude, she looked like a very incarnation of youth and loveliness. She was dressed in white muslin, which looked none the worse for the limpness caused by contact with John's wet clothing. Captain Hamilton gazed at her with a dawning admiration which seemed mixed with amaze. He had, of course, seen the child's mother previously, but, preoccupied by the condition of his soused garments, he had not realized the fact of her beauty.

"I am very glad I was able to be of some little assistance," he said, becoming amiable all at once. He had just been remarking to himself that the whole thing was an infernal bore. It had not even

the merit of recommending him in the eyes of anybody of importance; Frances's heart was won already, and there was no need to attitudinize for her
benefit. But it occurred to him now that it was
rather pleasant to hear this pretty provincial little
woman expressing her gratitude, and that she
looked as if one might get some amusement out
of her. In this dull place, Captain Hamilton told
himself, even a carpenter's wife might be amusing.

"He is quite right now, quite safe, isn't he, Dr.
Miller? Oh, it was so good of you to jump into
the water and save him, wasn't it, Miss Lisle? Oh,
aren't you quite proud of him?"

Gideon felt, with a sudden twinge, that Emmy
had said just the wrong thing. Why should Frances
Lisle be proud of Captain Hamilton? He saw a
deepening pink flush upon that cameo-like, pure
face; he saw her eyes cast down in momentary confusion, and he irritably wished to himself that
Emmy's tongue would not run so fast. *She* was
quite happy, quite contented with what she had
said; evidently she thought she had said just the
proper thing, but neither Miss Lisle nor Captain
Hamilton looked quite pleased with the remark.

Frances turned instinctively to Gideon, while Emmy pursued her conversation with the Captain and the doctor. The disturbed expression passed at once from her face as she spoke to him.

" What a dear little boy he is! " she said.

The father's eye gleamed.

" Yes, he's a fine little chap," he answered, simply enough, but with evident satisfaction.

" And his name is John ? "

" John Gideon—the name," said Gideon shyly, " of the man in the book."

" The man in the book ? " Frances was mystified for a moment, then she remembered, and spoke eagerly : " Of course I know. I am glad you called the little boy after him."

" Nobody knows," said Gideon, lowering his voice, and casting an involuntary glance of guilt towards Emmy. Frances laughed a little at the glance, but her heart warmed to the man. It struck her that he must be lonely, in spite of his environment of friends and family.

" I have never forgotten him," she said with an instinct of sympathy. " We all remember him every Sunday, and on All Souls' Day."

"It is rather a good thing, that," said Gideon seriously. "I think he wanted to be remembered, poor old chap!"

Remembrance was a different thing in his eyes from what it was in hers. But they came no nearer to a mutual understanding, because at that moment Miss Lisle's carriage was announced, and the visitors rose to take leave.

"I can't express all I feel," Emmy was saying, "and my husband can't, either; but I hope you will not be offended with us if we say so little."

Captain Hamilton thought she had said a good deal, but he smiled and took instant advantage of Mrs. Blake's apology.

"I shall be amply repaid if you will allow me to come and inquire after him some day. I love children, and I should like to make acquaintance with your fine little boy."

"Oh, certainly; come whenever you like," cried Emmy in high delight. "We shall be always pleased to see you—always, I'm sure."

He bowed over her hand with an exaggeration of courtesy which struck Frances as mocking and unkind.

"How *could* you make fun of Mrs. Blake!" she said to him afterwards, with a little reproach in her tone.

"You have such sharp eyes," he answered laughingly; "a little too sharp, sometimes, don't you think? Mrs. Blake liked it; she thought it a homage to her beauty. What a pretty woman she is!"

"Is she not lovely!" said Frances, with so much heartfelt warmth that Captain Hamilton was a trifle disappointed. He would have thought it more natural for Frances, who was comparatively plain, to depreciate Mrs. Blake's good looks; and he said to himself impatiently that she was far too angelic for this wicked world, and that angelic women were a bore.

Poor Frances felt herself far from angelic, being not free from miserable doubts of George Hamilton's sincerity, and disposed to accuse him of paying too much attention to every woman he came across. Even these ghosts of suspicion gave her an agony of pain and self-reproach. It seemed to her that she must herself be evil-minded and low-thoughted if she could even conceive the possibility of his doing wrong. Ordinarily she was a fairly shrewd and quick-witted little person, but her love for this man, George Hamilton, had strangely blinded her eyes. He had come, as she knew, to woo and win her; there had never been any doubt about that. The match had been "arranged," because she had money and he had debts (though this she did not know), and an old name to support, and she had agreed to the proposal with all her heart, in her own rather sober and serious way. Hamilton was of an order that she knew, and yet there was something novel and entrancing about him. To her mind, it was wonderful that he should want to marry her. She was very happy on the whole, but she was not always at rest.

When the carriage drove away from the little house by the river, Gideon stood gravely at the door, and Emmy, beside him, sent nods and smiles after the departing guests. Carry Blake hovered in the background, rather curious as to the way in which her stepbrother was taking the occurrence; and faithful Uncle Obed had stolen upstairs to the sleeping child.

"What *will* Gideon say?" Carry was asking herself, conscious of equal guilt with Emmy in hav-

8

ing taken the boy on the river against his father's
will.

But Gideon had no time to say anything.

As soon as the carriage was out of sight, Emmy
turned, glanced at his face, then, with a cry that
was half a sob, half a laugh, threw herself into his
arms.

" Oh, Gideon! I was very naughty and disagree-
able to you, but I'm really very sorry now—I am
indeed. And our poor little Jacky! he might have
been drowned. Oh, it was dreadful!"

She hid her face on his shoulder and burst into
tears, genuine enough, although caused partly by
excitement, agitation, and a little fear. Gideon put
up his hand and stroked her hair. He had no
words, except a murmur of affection and solicitude.
He was only too thankful that Emmy was apparently repentant of her escapade.

" Oh, I suffered fearfully!" said Mrs. Blake, at
last drying her eyes. " To see the darling sink in
the water—my nerves got such a shock that I don't
think I shall get over it for a month! I screamed,
did I not, Carry ?"—in a tone of conscious merit.
" I screamed at the top of my voice."

"Yes, you did; and so did I," said Carry triumphantly. "And that was what made Captain Hamilton look round. If he hadn't been there, I am sure Jacky would have been drowned."

It was Gideon who frowned and flinched at the word. Emmy was too deeply interested in the details of the event that had really occurred to be impressed by a figment of the imagination. She did not see, as Gideon saw, in his mind's eye, a picture of little John lying cold and dripping in someone's arms, carried back dead to the cottage, where he had made the brightness of his father's life. The ghastliness of it turned Gideon absolutely sick. But Carry and Emmy prattled on undisturbed.

"Did no one on board try to save him?" he inquired grimly.

Emmy looked at her sister-in-law. It was Carry who replied.

"Not a single one. Mr. Chiltern went quite white and green, and said that he couldn't swim. And nobody else said anything. Oh! Johnny would have been drowned, that's certain, if Captain Hamilton had not been there."

"You see what a fine set of fellows your friends are," said Gideon, a little grimly.

Emmy tossed her head.

"They are as good as other people, I suppose. I never heard that you could swim yourself," she said.

"Should you have gone in after him if you had been there, Gid?" said Carry, her eyes gleaming. "I suppose you would; but, you see, the fellows on the boat weren't his father, so——"

"Do let us hear no more about it," said Gideon, with sudden irritation. "Tell Keziah to get the tea, for goodness' sake; and be thankful that the boy is alive."

"You needn't speak so cross," said Emmy; but she felt the need of some pacification, and went into the kitchen to hasten preparations for the evening meal. Gideon leaned against the window and looked out into the garden; while Carry, perched on the music-stool, swung her feet and regarded him inquisitively. She did not understand her step-brother at all.

"Who *is* Captain Hamilton?" he asked presently.

"Oh! don't you know? He is to marry that Miss Frances Lisle who was here to-day. It's all for her money—everybody says so; because she's quite plain, and he's such a splendid-looking gentleman."

"Miss Lisle plain?" said Gideon, in a puzzled voice.

"Why, of course she is plain, Gideon! Don't you know a plain person from a pretty one? Well, I must say that I think Emmy is thrown away on you! Look here, Emmy, he thinks Miss Lisle pretty—*Miss Lisle!*"

"I never said so," Gideon averred, in the old irritated voice. "I don't know whether she is pretty or plain. She has what people call—a nice face, I believe."

Emmy laughed derisively.

"Gideon has no taste," she said. "Do you know, he can't bear that pink and blue dress of mine that I got at Hull! They told me it was an exact copy of a French costume, and yet he doesn't care for it. I never think anything of Gideon's taste now."

"Why has this Miss Lisle got money, if her

sisters have not?" said Gideon, disregarding these accusations. "You know everything, Carry: tell me that."

The slight satire was quite lost upon Carry.

"Everybody knows," she said, "except you; and I sometimes think you are blind and deaf, Gideon. It was her old aunt and godmother who left her a fortune. It all came into her hands when she was twenty-one, and she is quite independent. She is twenty-three now. Some people expected her to give her money to the Church, or set up a hospital or something; but she wasn't quite so silly as that. She's going to marry Captain Hamilton, and, as he's over head and ears in debt, he will be glad of the money."

"She's a lucky girl," said Emmy wistfully.

Gideon turned to her with a sharp gesture of dissent.

"The luck's on his side," he said.

The girls laughed scornfully to each other; they almost thought that Gideon was a little mad at times.

Later in the evening, when Carry had gone home and he was in the garden smoking a pipe,

Emmy stole out to him in a gentler mood, and twined her hand in his arm.

"I won't go on the barge again, Gideon," she said softly.

"That's right."

"I shall always hate it now. Think what it would have been for me if Jacky had been drowned? It would have been terrible. And I could not help thinking when I saw him fall, 'What will Gideon say?' Gideon," pressing a little closer to him, "what should we have done?"

"I don't know," said Gideon brokenly; "don't talk of it, Emmy."

"I believe you would never have forgiven me," she said, with a petulant little laugh, in which there was the echo of a sob.

"I don't suppose I ever should," said Gideon.

He could not understand why she wrenched her hand out of his arm and ran back to the house without another word. He watched her slim white figure in the moonlight, and wondered a little at women's vagaries. He did not know that he had brought tears of real pain and passion to Emmy's eyes.

" He does not care one bit about me," she said to herself, as she began to undress herself in the semi-darkness of her room, where John lay asleep in his crib. " He cares only for the child."

She was wrong; Gideon loved her too, but perhaps at that moment the love of his child came first.

V.

"I ALWAYS said so," remarked Mrs. Blake, senior, in her most tragic tones. "I always told you that Enderbys was a poor lot, Gideon ; but you were so set on marrying Emmy Enderby, that there was no holding you back, and now——"

She paused significantly, and her silence said more than words. Any other woman would perhaps have shrunk from exciting the wrath that was plainly to be seen in Gideon's dark face, but Mrs. Blake was not wanting in courage. And she had that curious insensibility to the pain of others which comes from absolute want of sympathy.

She was sitting in the parlour of Riverside Cottage on an August evening. Bolt upright on a high chair, her ample silk skirts spread out carefully on each side of her, she looked a worthy occupant of the *bourgeois* little room, where the green "rep" was growing soiled and frayed, and the lilies and roses of the carpet were beginning to merge their violent contrasts of colour in a decent obscurity. Mrs. Blake had "come to call," and she had come on a Saturday evening, when she had expected, she said somewhat viciously, "to find Mrs. Gideon at home."

Obed was in the garden, performing his favourite function of nurse and caretaker to little John, and Emmy was out. It was this fact that had put Mrs. Blake out of temper. She was impelled to vent her anger in spiteful words against the girl, although she knew that Gideon was not likely to be a very patient listener. He stood in what was a favourite attitude with him: leaning against the window-frame, looking out into the garden. It was a careless, lounging pose, but as Mrs. Blake spoke she might have noticed that he gradually gathered himself up a little, and that the hand which had been hanging loosely at his side clenched itself. Signs of danger there, if Mrs. Blake had only understood.

"Well!" said Gideon, as she paused. "And now—what then?"

"You may well say 'What then?'" said Mrs. Blake, pursing up her lips. "Indeed, I don't know what is to become of you all; and my heart aches when I look at that poor child of yours and think how he is to be brought up with *such* parents. I hear that you never send him to Sunday-school, and that he does not come to church. I don't know how you expect him to grow up respectable."

"He's too young for church," said Gideon shortly. "He generally goes for a walk with me on Sundays. Emmy goes to church; Emmy and Uncle Obed do the religion of the family."

"Ah Emmy—Emmy!" said Mrs. Blake, with a portentous sigh. "Not much religion about *her*, I'm afraid. Perhaps it would be better if she had a little more."

"Look here," said Gideon suddenly, and with violence, "what do you mean by talking about Emmy in that tone? If you've anything to say, say it and be done with it. You seem rather to forget that Emmy's my wife."

"Ah, poor thing! yes. I'm sorry for you, Gideon. I should have wished you a good wife, I

should indeed: for the unbelieving husband may be
sanctified by the believing wife——"

"Are you insinuating that Emmy is not a good
wife?" said Gideon sternly.

"Insinuating? What a long word!" said Mrs.
Blake, with acidulated playfulness. "No, I am not
insinuating anything, or, at least, not more than
everyone is saying, and I am not responsible, I
hope, for what other people say."

"What do they say?"

He left the window-frame and looked at her,
his face paling beneath its summer tan, his breath
coming faster than usual. Mrs. Blake was proud
of having made such an impression. Her big
teeth gleamed and gave her a hungry look as she
replied:

"They talk, Gideon—of course they talk.
When a young wife neglects her home and her
husband——"

"It will be time enough to talk of her neglect-
ing me when *I* complain."

"Of course. And it is very forbearing of
you not to complain more than you do. I'm
sure I never gave you credit, Gideon, for such

patience. But I believe you *were* fond of Emmy——"

"*Were!*"

The exclamation was so indignant, the tone so full of scorn and anger, that even Mrs. Blake felt a little thrill of alarm.

"Well, you *are* fond of her, then, if you like that better. There is such a thing as being weak and blind in one's fondness, but I don't wish to 'insinuate' anything, as you call it. I'm not one to make mischief. Ever since I was a girl I've taken for my motto the text 'Blessed are the peacemakers.'"

"You make peace in a damned extraordinary way," said Gideon, flaming into sudden rage. "I'd as soon be without it, for my part."

"Oh, if you mean to swear at me, Gideon," said Mrs. Blake, drawing herself up with dignity, "I can only say that I shall never set foot in your house again. I am not accustomed to be sworn at. It's a thing your father never did, and where you learned it I am sure I cannot tell; and my own father was a most respectable man, and wouldn't have sullied his lips with a bad word,

more especially to a lady and one that had come to
call and was anxious for his soul's good.   Which
is what I have always been, although from the
very first moment that I entered your father's
house you took a grudge against me—and showed
it.   But I hope I am a Christian woman, and
always ready to do you a good turn when it comes
in my way."

This long speech gave Gideon time in which
to recover himself.   He fell back against the window-frame and folded his arms.   His face was in
shadow, but his voice had grown calm again when
he made answer:

"I beg your pardon.   I did not mean to hurt
your feelings, I am sure.   But you must see"—
with a little gathering vehemence—"that a man
doesn't like to be told that his wife neglects him
or anything of that kind.   It's not likely."

"No, indeed, it's not likely that one always
cares to hear the truth," said Mrs. Blake sharply;
"but it may be your friends' duty to let you know
it, for all that.   In plain words, Gideon, your
wife gads about too much, and I should advise
you to look after her."

"Is that what you came to say?" asked Gideon, who was at a white heat.

"Well, I came to say a word to Emmy, and that's the truth. I should have said a deal more to her than I've said to you, Gideon. But as Emmy's as usual out and about, flaunting all over the town——"

"Take care what you say," cried the young man fiercely.

"Really, Gideon," said Mrs. Blake, shaking out her silk skirts as she rose to go, "I don't see that I've said anything that calls for that tone of voice. I don't approve of so much gadding about, of course; but I have not said, as I might have said, that when it comes to strolls by the river with that Captain Hamilton up at the Park——"

She ceased suddenly: Gideon's hand was on her arm, his dark eyes were flashing fire. His voice was so husky that she could hardly recognise it as that of her step-son.

"Dare to say anything against my wife," he said in a choking whisper, "dare to breathe a word against her, and I'll—I'll *murder* you!"

His voice and face were so frightful to Mrs.

Blake that she uttered a faint, terrified shriek, and sped trembling to the door. He let her go, but before she had left the room she heard him say in a stronger, steadier voice:

"Never enter this house again."

"Indeed I won't," said Mrs. Blake, unwilling to depart without at least one Parthian shot, "and for why—because no respectable person in Casterby will care to enter it, either, when your wife has lost her character."

She shut the door after her as she said the last words, and perhaps it was as well, for Gideon threw himself forward as if to hasten her departure by forcible means. The closed door, however, restrained him. He stood before it silent and motionless for a moment, then, with an impatient gesture, he turned back to the window and leaned once more against the frame.

At first his face and bearing expressed nothing but wrath; his eyes gleamed under the dark brows, and his hands clenched themselves; he muttered angry words to himself against gossiping women and scandalous tongues. When he grew calmer, an expression of anxious doubt crept into his eyes;

his face grew intensely gloomy, as if his mind were visited with dismal forebodings. Then a fit of restlessness came upon him: he walked up and down the room, looked at his watch, went upstairs and down again; finally walked out into the garden, and approached the wooden bench where Obed Pilcher sat, peacefully smoking a long clay pipe. Beside him John was busy digging with a small spade in one of the garden-beds.

Gideon halted irresolutely near the old man and the child. Obed asked him the very question that he dreaded to hear.

"Where's Emmy?" he said.

"Gone out. I don't know where."

There was a suppressed pain and impatience in his voice which made Uncle Obed look at him keenly. He had seen Mrs. Blake's hurried departure. "Reckon t' owd wumman has been sayin' summat she needn't ha' said," he remarked to himself. Then, in an unconscious tone:

"Mebbe Emmy's gone to see her mother."

"Yes; that's it. Of course she has," said Gideon, with eager assent and relief. His face cleared at the comforting reflection. He seated

9

himself on the garden bench, and asked John what he was doing.

"I be diggin' a girt hole," said John, whose accent had been acquired mainly from Uncle Obed—much to Emmy's disgust. He stopped his work, and leaned on his spade, looking at his father solemnly. For his age he spoke with remarkable clearness.

"Ay, and what's the hole for?"

"To get *frough*—to the ozzer side of the world," said John, with determination.

"Ah, I remember beginning to do that once," said Gideon, with a laugh.

"Did oo get frough?" asked John, with interest.

"No. It had to be such a big hole that I got tired and left off."

"I san't get tired," said John sturdily.

He resumed his digging, and the father and the uncle watched him with the silent adoration for which Emmy often laughed at them both.

"He's a fine lad," said Uncle Obed.

Gideon nodded, without speaking.

"But he's noan so stout as he looks. He's a

bit like Ruth—your mother, Gid. She died of a chest complaint."

"John's as strong as a little pony," said Gideon.

"He's had a bit of a cough ever sin' he fell into t' watter," said Uncle Obed gloomily.

"Rubbish!" said his nephew. Then, in an uneasy tone: "I'll tell Miller to look at him again. But Emmy thinks he's all right."

"Emmy's nobbut a wumman, after all," said Obed philosophically, "and women is all alike at boddom. A poor sort, mostly. I doan't think mooch o' any wumman I ever saw. Ruth was t' best; but she's dead, poor soul!"

"I never can see why you should say 'poor soul' because she's dead," said Gideon, with a touch of the crabbed gloom to which he was sometimes subject.

"Eh," said Obed, "it's because we know what we have to bear, living, but not what we come to when we're dead."

"I'm tired," said John, flinging down his spade. "I can't get frough to-night, fazer. I fink I would raver go to bed."

He clambered on Gideon's knee, and pressed his soft lips to his father's cheek. Gideon held him close, perhaps too close, for John wriggled himself free and began to cough. It was rather a hoarse little cough, which Gideon remembered that he had heard before. It went through him like a knife.

"Eh! don't cough," he said, almost sharply in his agony. "Have you a cold?"

"No," said John. "I always cough like that in the evenin'-time."

"Mother must give you some lozenges and put you to bed," said Gideon.

Where *was* mother? Why did she not come home and nurse her child? Had she no love for him, as that chattering woman had implied?

"Mammy tells me not to make a noise," said John sleepily. "An' ze man what pulled me out of ze river makes faces at me."

Gideon's brow contracted. He started up.

"Come, John, I'll take you to bed. Go to sleep, and don't cough any more. Say good-night to Uncle Obed."

"I be a-gooin' down to th' church," said

Obed. "There's a practice or summat agate. Good-bye, lad. I'll be hoame by ten, Gideon."

He hobbled away, and Gideon carried the boy into the house, undressed him with tender, awkward fingers, and put him into his little crib. Those who knew him as a man of morose and sullen disposition, with, as was popularly believed, a violent and unbridled temper, might have wondered to see him caring in this way for his child—unfastening strings and buttons, listening to the sleepily-uttered little prayers, sitting beside the small cot until its occupant fell fast asleep. Throughout all, the dark face preserved its wonderfully softened expression; but when at last, as the light of day faded, he rose to go downstairs, it grew hard again—hard and set and grim.

Emmy had not come in yet. Supper was laid in the little dull dining-room, but Gideon did not touch the food that was set out. He went into the garden, and stood at the gate listening and looking. The maid-servant had gone to see her relations. Gideon and John were alone in the house.

At last she came, but not from the town. Gideon noticed that at once. She came from the other side of the garden, as if she had been walking along the river-bank, and she was running instead of walking, as if she were afraid of being late. When she saw Gideon, she dropped into a walk, and began to hum a little tune, meaning thereby that she was neither excited nor in haste; but even in that dim light Gideon saw that her cheeks were flushed and her eyes glistening like stars.

"Where have you been?" he asked abruptly.

She stopped short at the gate and looked at him, laughing nervously.

"I've been into the town to see mother, of course," she said. "And she kept me talking so long that I was afraid you would want your supper, so I hurried home to give it you. Now, wasn't that good of me?"

Gideon did not often mince his words. He lifted his heavy eyes to her face and looked straight into hers.

"You lie!" he said.

Emmy recoiled a little, as if he had struck her with his hand.

"Gideon, what a brute you are!" she said, in a tone of sharp exasperation. "I *have* been to mother's; you can go and ask her if you like."

" Yes, but she did not keep you late, and you have not come straight from her house. Why do you tell me what is not true? What is it you are keeping back?"

He had all but turned his stepmother out of the house for her insinuations against Emmy's good name; nevertheless, suspicion had taken hold of him, and made him fierce and wild.

" Why should I be keeping anything back?" she asked, eluding a direct answer, as he very quickly noticed. "I have been to mother's . . . and then I just ran down to the water-path to look for a glow-worm that I saw shining in the grass. I thought it would amuse Jacky. Is there anything dreadful in that?"

" There is more than that," said Gideon slowly.

His face showed white and grim in the twilight, and the colour began to die out of Emmy's cheeks. "I have been told—to-night—that people talk about you; they say that you spend your time gadding about—that you do not love your husband and your child any longer——"

"Who says such horrid things?" said Emmy indignantly.

Then a sob caught her voice; she put her hand up to her throat and looked away.

"It does not matter who says them so long as they are not true," said Gideon. "Oh, Emmy, tell me—say that it is not true—you do love me still?"

The passion in his voice touched her, but she did not want to show that she was touched. She shifted from one foot to the other, shook her slim shoulders, turned her head to the dim landscape beyond the garden, so that she should not see Gideon's face.

"It is silly to talk in this way," she broke out at length, "when we are old married people, who have got over all that nonsense about love! What on earth should we talk about it for?"

"Because I shall never get over it—because I care about it more than anything in the world beside," said Gideon, in a low, passionate voice.

"You were always foolish," she said, with a cold laugh, "always different to other people. Other men don't trouble—don't bother themselves——"

"Don't trouble whether their wives are false or true?"

There was the old fierceness in his tone.

"It's nothing to do with being false or true," said Emmy, and he saw a sudden flush of colour in her face; "it's only a question of my going out to tea oftener than you like, and running down to mother's. You are selfish—that's what it is; you want to keep me cooped up here, in this miserable little house, until I feel inclined to throw myself into the river. *You* get plenty of change and amusement, but I get none."

Were these entirely her own opinions, or were they adopted from the lips of someone else? It seemed to Gideon that they had not quite a natural ring. He wondered dully whether she had read them in a book.

"You—get—none?" he repeated. He was almost stunned by the accusation.

"Well, what do I get?" asked Emmy, raising her voice defiantly. "You grumble and scold if I go out with my friends or run down to mother's. You never take me anywhere from one year's end to another. Other people go to Scarborough or

Bridlington, but we go nowhere. I would not even mind Cleethorpes; it would be a change. But you never seem to think of such a thing."

"I haven't been quite well able to afford it, as you know," said Gideon, who had thrust his hands into his pockets and was staring gloomily at the ground. "And—I didn't know you wanted it—as much as all that."

"Will you take me this year, then?" said Emmy pantingly. "Do, Gideon, do; I *want* to go."

There was a note of pleading pain in her voice which was new to Gideon, but he did not understand what it implied.

"I can't; it is impossible," he said, plunging his hands deeper into his pockets, and frowning darkly.

He could not bring himself at that moment to tell her that he was unable to afford a seaside jaunt because he had advanced every available pound of his own earnings to free his father from a mortgage which the holder threatened to foreclose. He felt vaguely that the knowledge of this fact ought to exculpate him, even in Emmy's eyes; but he had an unreasonable dislike to making excuses for him-

self, especially at the expense of other people.
Therefore, he was silent, and Emmy made a gesture
of anger and disgust.

"It's always so!" she said. "Whenever I want
anything particularly, it's always the same old story
—no money! no money! If I had known you were
going to be so poor, do you think I would have
married you? To live in this hovel of a place, and
go nowhere and see nobody? Not I! But it .isn't
poverty, it's meanness, and that is what makes me
angry. I hate a mean man."

"Are you calling *me* mean?" said Gideon
slowly.

"Yes, I am. Are you so stupid that you can't
take even that in? Yes; you are as mean as anyone can be, for you won't spend your money even
on your wife and child. Where does it all go to?
You've no house-rent to pay, because your uncle
gives us house-room; and a miserable arrangement
it is, to have that vulgar old man always prying
about——"

"Stop that, Emmy!" said Gideon, roused to
decision by her abuse of poor old Uncle Obed.
"I'll not hear a word against *him*."

"Oh, of course, your relations are perfect," she mocked. "But you're the only person that finds them so. Mother always told me I—I was making a mistake." Her voice began to choke, and the tears to gather in her eyes. "But I ne—never thought—you would be so—unkind."

"Unkind, am I?" Gideon said, recovering the grimness of manner which showed that he was displeased. "Well, there may be two opinions about that, you know. I've only this to say: you must be content to stay at home. I won't have people talking about my wife, and saying that she is a gad-about; least of all"—and his voice hardened—"will I have them saying that you take walks with Captain Hamilton."

Emmy had been quietly crying, but at these words her eyes blazed, and the hot colour leaped into her wet cheeks.

"Who says so?" she gasped. "Who tells such *lies* about me?"

"Are they lies?" said Gideon, looking straight at her.

"I may have seen him once or twice when I was out with John," said Emmy in a beaten voice, "and he always stops to speak to John : he takes such an interest in him ever since he pulled him out of the river. You ought to like him for that."

" I'm grateful to him for saving the boy's life," said Gideon—"I can't be less, I suppose ; but all the same, I won't have him hanging about my house and my wife, and making foolish people say unkind things of you."

" He does no harm."

" I don't suppose he does. I should kill him if I thought he meant any harm—and you, too."

" Oh, Gideon ! "

But she was subtly flattered by the threat.

" So you may tell him to keep away if he ever comes here again."

" I can't do that, Gideon ; it would look so rude and unkind," she murmured faintly.

" Then, you must keep out of his way. You need not speak to him if you meet him."

" I can't make myself ridiculous," said Emmy sullenly. "One would think you were jealous, Gideon. I should hope I could look after my-self."

"It seems you can't, as you've made yourself

town-talk already," her husband replied bitterly. " But for the future you'll do as I tell you."

There was a little silence. Gideon had said all that he had wanted to say. Emmy had reached the point where she knew protestation to be useless. She took out her handkerchief, and wiped away some tears, as she stood with her back to the garden-gate.

Gideon, on the other side, was not insensible to this mute appeal. After a few moments, he leaned over the gate and put his arms round her waist.

" Emmy, look at me! Don't cry, my darling; I didn't mean to be unkind."

" You were —very unkind," sobbed Emmy, pursuing an undoubted advantage.

" I am very sorry. Won't you forgive me? I didn't mean it; and I'll see what we can do about Scarborough. Perhaps you and John could go there without me for a little while. John does not seem quite well——"

" Oh, you can afford it when its a question of John's health; but not when it only affects my happiness!" cried Emmy, repulsing him.

He lingered, mute and bewildered, for a minute

or two, then would have spoken again and renewed his caresses, had not Emmy pushed him aside, slipped through the gate, and hidden herself in the house, where, from the lights in the windows, he was soon able to conjecture that she had betaken herself to bed.

He had a sore and a heavy heart, and he could not tell himself that he had bettered matters by speaking; for Emmy was very cold to him after that day, and went out more than ever, in complete defiance of his expressed desire.

VI.

"Here I and Sorrow sit."

THE autumn at Casterby grew wild and wet, after the glorious summer. Emmy went out less, and was quieter than usual. She refused to go to Scarborough with John, as Gideon proposed to her to do; but she made occasional excursions to a small seaside place at a short distance from Casterby, and returned thence with an excitement of manner which struck Gideon as inexplicable. He would almost rather that she had gone to Scarborough with John, for the boy's health seemed delicate, and the father was anxious about him. But Emmy laughed his anxiety to scorn.

The breach between Mrs. Blake, senior, and her stepson was healed, for Mrs. Blake had apologized (somewhat reluctantly) for her insinuations, and Gideon was too much attached to his father to be implacable. So it happened that he went to his father's house to tea one afternoon in October, for Emmy was to meet him there and to walk home with him afterwards. Obed remained at home with the boy.

They were all seated at the tea-table when Gideon arrived. He hung up his hat in the hall, and waited a moment to let a maidservant pass him with a tray. It was cold and wet and dark, and the gas was already lighted in the dining-room, from which came the sound of women's tongues, and the scent of tea, hot cakes, and eau-de-Cologne. As he waited, a piece of news floated to his ears.

"Oh yes, it's all broken off," said the voice of a guest. "I understand that Captain Hamilton is going back to London directly."

"You'll *miss him*, dear," said another voice sweetly.

To whom could she be speaking? And why were the words followed by such an ominous little silence? Gideon stepped into the room in rather a curious mood.

But he forgot the subject—it was one of no importance—when he looked at Emmy's face, the

10

point to which his eyes always travelled first when he came into a room. What was the matter with Emmy? for something had vexed her without a doubt. Her cheeks were as scarlet as poppies, and the tears did not seem far from her forget-me-not eyes. There was an unmistakable frown upon her brow, a pout upon her lips. The voices, which had suddenly ceased even before Gideon's entrance, now took up their strain once more, and Emmy was the only person who sat silent in the company. But when Gideon, looking persistently at her, attracted her attention, she gave him an unusually bright smile and a friendly nod, and entered into conversation with her neighbours with such spirit that Gideon felt relieved. He had certainly thought that Emmy was seriously embarrassed and annoyed.

As he had come late, he was not put in any seat of honour, but found himself close to his stepsister Carry, a position of which he did not altogether approve. By way of making talk, he asked her unconcernedly:

" *Whose* engagement has been broken off?"

" Miss Lisle's, of course," said Carry promptly.

"Oh! how's that?" asked Gideon, helping himself to the hot cakes.

"Well, they say it's because she has lost all her money and he won't have her," said Carry; "but I don't think anybody knows exactly."

"He's a cur, if he won't marry her because she has lost her money," said Gideon carelessly, "but I hope it's not that."

"Perhaps he has seen somebody he likes better," said Carry demurely.

In the midst of the dialogue, across the buzz of conversation that seemed to fill the room, came Emmy's voice, high and sharp across the lower tones, as she addressed her husband and her sister-in-law from the other side of the table.

"You are very ready to speak evil of people you know nothing about, I think," she said, with red cheeks and sparkling eyes. "Captain Hamilton would never have given her up for the loss of her money; it was because he found he did not love her that he gave her up."

The eyes of the company were fixed on Emmy in rather a curious way.

"How do *you* know?" said Carry's small, shrill pipe.

And Gideon looked at his wife in simple amazement.

"Oh—I know, because—somebody told me so," she answered angrily. "And Captain Hamilton saved Jacky's life, and I—I never like to hear him run down."

"No, of course not—of course not, my dear," said old Joe Blake, in a soothing tone. Emmy was sitting next to him, and he laid his big hand over hers and patted it. "You are quite right to stick up for the man who saved your boy's life," he said; and Gideon felt grateful to him for saying it.

The clash of gossiping tongues began again; the reek of smoking teapots and muffins filled the air. Attention was diverted from Emmy, who felt ashamed of her outbreak; but Gideon's eye was fixed thoughtfully upon her, and—horror of horrors! —she felt the big tears beginning to fall. Two splashed straight into her lap, a choking sensation came in her throat, and she wondered whether she were going to faint. Then, fortunately for her,

came the move to the "best room." She was able
to breathe a cooler air, and to fly upstairs to bathe
her face; and in a little while she was downstairs
again, seated at the piano, and singing the most
popular song of the hour at the very top of her
voice.

Gideon was not of a sociable turn, and he wanted
to be home again, for John had caught a feverish
cold, which made the father anxious. However, he
knew that there was no use in trying to hasten
Emmy's departure, and he therefore waited patiently, standing about in corners with crossed arms
and an air of resignation which some people thought
sullen. Emmy was the life of the party. With
blazing cheeks and brilliant, dilated eyes, she was
the centre of every amusement which Casterby
ideas of propriety allowed at an evening entertainment. There was, of course, no dancing, but there
were round games of various kinds, and a charade
at the close of the evening. It was nearly twelve
o'clock when the guests went home.

"Oh, I am so tired!" said Emmy, as soon as she
had quitted the house and turned into the broad wet
street. Her vivacity fell from her like a garment,

and left her petulant and dissatisfied. "Fancy having to walk all this way!"

"I'm sorry it's raining," said Gideon in an apologetic way, as though he were responsible for the weather; "but we shall soon be home now. I wonder how John is?"

"Oh, John! John!" she repeated irritably. "You care for nobody but John."

"You have no right to say that," said Gideon, not wise enough to know that silence was his best policy. "You are always making accusations of that sort, and yet surely you are fond of John yourself. At least, I suppose you are, or you would not make such a fuss about that Captain Hamilton for saving him."

This was carrying the war into the enemy's country indeed. Emmy wrenched her arm away from him, and walked on the other side of the pavement. He followed her with the umbrella which he had been holding over both their heads, and half regretted his speech, for he saw that her lips were quivering and her eyes ready to overflow. But she did not reply, and for some minutes they walked on in silence.

"We seem to be always wrangling, now," said Emmy at last, in a heart-broken voice, "and nothing I do or say is right. I'm sure I don't know how it is. I think you would be happier without me."

"Don't be a fool!" said Gideon gruffly.

"Oh, I'm not such a fool as you think. I can see that you are wrapped up in the child, and think nothing of me."

"*Your* child, Emmy," said her husband, a touch of deep feeling showing itself beneath his usual reserve.

"He's taken my place, any way," she answered obstinately; and against this extraordinary assertion Gideon felt himself powerless to strive. He tried to change the subject.

"It was a nice sort of party, wasn't it?" he said, a little doubtfully.

"It was a horrible, hateful party," said Emmy, with sudden fire, "and I can't think why I ever went to it. Silly little tea-parties in a country town, what are they? If it had been a big ball, such as one reads of in books, or a stately dinner-party—but what can you expect in a little place like this?"

"But even if we lived in a bigger place," said Gideon, "you know, my dear, we should not have the chance of those things."

She made an impatient movement.

"Oh, I know as well as you do," she said, "the shamefully sordid, poverty-stricken life we are likely to lead. And I don't suppose you would have done any better for me if you could. I'm tired of it."

Gideon made no answer. His temper was not under much control, but Emmy's direct attacks pained rather than angered him. His love for her gave him a kind of patience, which he showed to no one else. Neither of them spoke another word until they reached the house, when a few cold and trivial remarks on John's condition were interchanged.

John was not well. He was coughing a good deal and very feverish. The following morning was Saturday, and Gideon left him in bed, promising that he would come home early and sit with him all the afternoon. He thought that Emmy looked at him oddly as he said the words.

"Are you going out?" he asked her.

She turned away hastily.

"No—at least, I may run down to mother's. If you are with Jacky, he will be all right—I needn't stay in."

"No. I only thought you would hardly care to leave him."

"I don't make myself such a slave to the child as you do," said Emmy scornfully. "He would be all right if he was up and out; it's a lovely day."

Indeed, the sun was shining brilliantly, and the yellowing leaves of the trees looked golden in the light. The garden was full of autumn flowers—chrysanthemums and sunflowers and Michaelmas daisies; it looked quite attractive to John's childish eyes as he lay in his crib near the window. He noted what his mother said, but was shrewd enough not to provoke discussion; he had already learnt wisdom in these matters. When his father was gone out he spoke.

"Mammy, may I get up? I'm tired of being in bed."

"Oh yes; get up if you like," said Emmy carelessly. She was trying the effect of ribbons against her face in the glass. As John scrambled into his garments, without much assistance from her, he wondered at the pretty things that she took out from her drawers and looked at now and then. Once he caught the glitter of stones and gold, and pressed nearer to see. "Oh, let me look!" he cried. He could not understand why his mother turned round angrily and boxed his ears: he did not know that he was doing anything wrong. She seemed to want to get him out of the room, so he crept downstairs to the kitchen, where Keziah, the maid-of-all-work, consoled him and gave him a lemon cheesecake. But he was not hungry, and after holding it for some time in his hand, he put it down, and strolled out of the kitchen into the parlour, where it was not so hot and stifling as it was by the kitchen fire.

Emmy came downstairs, and found him curled up in a nest of cushions on the sofa, with the cat on his lap. She took no notice of his flushed face and heavy eyes, nor of the croupy cough which shook his little frame every few minutes; she had matters of her own to think of which completely absorbed her mind. She was dressed for walking, with a rather thick veil tied over her face; but through the black net it could be seen that there were hot spots of colour on her cheeks, and that her eyes were unusually bright. Her voice had a strained, unnatural tension as she spoke.

"John, what business have you here? However, it doesn't matter. I'm going out; tell father I shan't be home till—late."

"Where's oo goin', mammy?" said John hoarsely.

"Oh, I'm going to see a friend. I'm going by train."

"Give me a kiss, mammy," said the child, rousing himself up and tumbling the cat off his lap in his haste. "You *always* kiss Jacky good-bye."

She came and stooped down to kiss him, and when she felt the baby arms round her neck she began to quiver and to sob.

"Oh, Jacky—mother's little Jacky—how can I go away?" she cried, with her face on the soft little neck.

"Stay, then, mammy—stay with Jacky; he's so poorly. Stay and make him well."

Emmy knelt beside him for a moment, and he

felt her trembling in every limb; then, as if by a supreme effort, she rose and drew herself away.

"How silly I am!" she said impatiently. "You won't want me, John; you have father and Uncle Obed and Keziah: you'll be all right. Good-bye; take care of yourself."

She went out without looking back. In the hall she stopped and called to the maid, still in the same strained, high voice:

"Keziah! Look after John, will you?"

"Are you going out, m'm?" said Keziah stolidly.

"Yes; I'm going to Hull, to do some shopping. You can tell master so when he comes in. I shall not be home till late."

"There ain't nothing ordered for Sunday dinner," said Keziah in a resentful tone. "And you haven't made the pies nor nothing. Master won't be main pleased if we give him rice pudden again——"

"Oh, be quiet with your puddings and pies," said Emmy, putting up her hands to her ears. "It's always the way—always a talk about housekeeping and cooking—till I'm sick of it. Get what you like ; I don't care."

She turned to the front-door, and Keziah retired grumbling to the kitchen. A little figure stood at the parlour-door—a little figure with tousled fair head and feverish lips, calling hoarsely to "mammy" for a parting word.

"Mammy, may I sit up till oo come back ?" the little cracked voice said.

It was with a movement of absolute desperation that Emmy opened the door and slid out into the garden, shutting her ear to Jacky's plaintive little cry "Oh, why didn't I go at night?" she was saying to herself, "when the child was asleep, and couldn't plague me in this way!" A sob escaped her lips. "He'll never plague me again," she said to herself. Then a wave of bitterness checked the sobs. "They'll forget me easily enough; Gideon simply worships the boy, and doesn't care a bit about me. Well, he will see now that somebody else is willing to give up everything for my sake— just as I am giving up everything for his. Not that I have very much to give up," she added, laughing a little wildly as she shut the garden-gate behind her. "Oh, I wish it was all over; I wish I were safe in London—with George! *He'll* protect me—*he'll* take care of me. I shall never know another care."

Here the connected line of thought was broken, for she had turned out of the lane into the main street of the town. She would willingly have avoided it, but there was no other way of getting to the station, where she meant to take a train to Retford. At Retford she was to book for London, but she had been counselled not to take her London ticket from Casterby, as she might be more easily tracked if the direction of her journey were known. And she had no desire to be followed, just as she had no desire ever to return to Casterby.

Just as she turned into the road an open carriage passed by. The horses were going at a footpace, and the carriage had only one occupant, whom Emmy recognised as Miss Frances Lisle. The two women looked each other straight in the face, but, for some reason or other, neither of them betrayed any sign of recognition. Frances was very pale, and her face had a drawn look, but her eyes rested steadily and calmly on the heated, excited counte-

nance that Emmy showed behind her veil. There
was an air of triumph, of exultation, about Mrs.
Blake which Frances remembered afterwards. The
carriage passed slowly forward, and Emmy sped
with hurried footsteps to the railway station, where
she took her ticket unobserved, and was quickly
borne away from Casterby.

Gideon came home about two o'clock, and was
horrified to see John's face at the door.

"What are you doing out of bed?" he exclaimed, almost roughly.

"Mammy said I might get up," answered the
boy. "An' my cough's not so drefful bad now, I
fink. I'm so glad you've comed, daddy. It's been
so *werry* lonely."

"Has mother gone out, then?" said Gideon, in
a startled voice.

"She's gone to do shopping. She won't be
back till late."

"Missis has gone to Hull," said Keziah, appear-
ing at the kitchen door with a melancholy face.
"And nothing ordered for to-morrow! She said I
was to ask you what you'd have."

"Oh, I don't care," said Gideon, gathering John up into his arms. "Get what you like; I dare say it will be all right. Roast beef and plum pie—that's the usual sort of thing, isn't it? And you, young man, you must come in out of the cold. Ah, coughing again! You ought to be in bed."

"Mammy didn't want to go away," said John irrelevantly. "She kied when she kissed me, she did."

"That must have been because you had a cough," said Gideon cheerfully, though he knitted his brow over John's statement.

After dinner, which was a very scrappy meal, he made Keziah light the fire in the sitting-room, a task at which she grumbled a good deal, and drew up the couch to the hearth with all a man's disregard for conventional arrangements of the furniture. Here Uncle Obed joined them before long, and the two men devoted themselves with somewhat pathetic solicitude to the entertainment of the sick child. They had a difficult task, for John was in the restless, petulant state of approaching illness, and would not be pleased with anything. All his toys were strewn on the floor;

every picture-book in the house had been brought out for his amusement; and Gideon had roared himself as hoarse as the child in his successive impersonations of lions and bears, but without much result; for, with the perversity of childhood and of sickness, John took it into his head to cry for his mother, and to declare that he wanted nobody but her.

Crying made him cough again, and his hands were so hot and dry that Gideon at last whispered to his uncle to go for Dr. Miller. The doctor appeared between six and seven o'clock, when the light was beginning to fade, and found Gideon walking up and down the firelit room with the child in his arms. John had sunk into a doze, but when he was roused he looked about him with glazed eyes which seemed to see nothing, and babbled of his mother.

"Eh, where is his mother, by the way?" the doctor asked.

"I expect her back every minute," said Gideon, not taking his eyes from John's face. "She went to do some shopping at Hull to-day, unfortunately."

11

"Nay, my good man, she didn't do that," said Dr. Miller good-humouredly, and not meaning any harm. "I saw her at Gainsborough Station this afternoon."

"Oh, well, it's all the same; she's gone to buy things," said Gideon impatiently. "What does it matter? Just look at the boy, doctor, and tell me what's wrong with him."

The doctor drew in his lips with a smothered whistle. He had not only seen Mrs. Blake at Gainsborough, but he had noticed that she was in the Retford train. Was Gideon not aware of the fact? The doctor did not want to make mischief, and therefore said nothing more just then. He turned his attention to the boy.

"Yes, you must get him to bed," he said, rather gravely, after examining him. "I hope it won't turn to pneumonia. What will you do for a nurse?"

"We can nurse him well enough, Emmy and I," said Gideon.

"Do you think she will get back—from Retford—to-night?"

"Retford!"

"My dear Gideon, I dare say she had got into the Retford train by mistake. I saw her in the carriage, and wondered what she was off to Retford for. But if she went there to do her shopping, she will hardly get back to-night."

Gideon had turned pale. He made a step towards the door as if he meant to rush off in search of his wife; then his eyes fell on John's flushed face, and he stopped short.

"I can't leave the boy," he said, with a glance towards the doctor that was almost piteous. His hands trembled, and the doctor bit his lip.

"It's all right, no doubt," said the rough, kindly little man. "She's made a mistake in the train, and will come flying back in great tribulation before long, or will send a telegram saying that she can't get back to-night.. Awkward, when your boy's ill, but it can't be helped. Shall I go round to Mrs. Worlaby's and ask her to look in for the night?"

Mrs. Worlaby was a nurse. Gideon resented the suggestion.

"I don't suppose there's anything *she* can do that I can't," he said sourly.

"H'm, I don't know. Can you make a poultice, for example?"

"No, but Keziah can."

"Keziah. Let me see—Keziah Wragge. Yes, she comes of a nursing family; perhaps she can manage. I will speak to her. And do you get that boy to bed."

The doctor strode out into the kitchen, and Gideon, seizing a rug from the sofa, wrapped the child in its soft folds and carried him upstairs. Here he found Obed Pilcher on his knees before the little bedroom grate, where he was already lighting a fire. Unfortunately, the chimney had been stuffed up, and wanted cleaning, and even when a bundle of straw had been removed it did not "draw" very well; the consequence was that successive puffs of smoke soon filled the room, thickening the atmosphere, and making John cough and cry.

"Doan't thee cry now, sonny," said Obed cheerfully. "Smoake 'll soon go, an' then theer'll be a nice bit o' fire. Sithee now, 'tis better already."

"Oh, this won't do!" said the doctor, coming

in abruptly and snuffing up the smoke. "This is intolerable!"

He glanced round sharply, as if to scold some-one, and then stopped short, taking in the elements of the scene. There was Obed Pilcher, bending his rheumatic knees and half breaking his old back, in trying to make the fire burn up. There was Gideon, sitting on the bed, with the sick child—only the doctor knew how sick—held close to his breast. A vision of Emmy floated before Dr. Miller's mind, and—whether she came back, or whether she had gone altogether, as he shrewdly suspected—he felt certain that only unhappiness and misery could follow in her train. He was sorry for all of them—sorry for the old man, panting and grunting over the smoking hearth; sorry for the little boy, in his feverish pain and weakness; sorry most of all for Gideon, whose look of mute endurance touched the doctor to the heart.

He scolded no longer, but applied himself ener-getically to the task of setting things in order. Dr. Miller was a man of resource. He suggested that, as there was already a comfortable fire in the par-lour, the child's bed should be made there at once.

He helped Keziah to make and apply a poultice; he fetched a bronchitis-kettle from home with his own hands, and did not leave the cottage until he had seen all arrangements made for a brave fight with the malady which had attacked the child. At the last moment Obed Pilcher took heart of grace, and tremulously asked the question which Gideon had tacitly avoided.

" Is it serious, doctor ? " said the old man, looking into Dr. Miller's face.

" All children's complaints are serious," said the doctor dogmatically. "Their temperature goes up and down so quickly that they want great care. *But*, with care, there is no reason why any complaint should not be cured, if taken in time."

With this enigmatic reply he took his departure, calling out to Obed to send for him if the child should be worse. And then the two men set themselves to wrestle with the enemy all the long night through—to wrestle with the Angel of Death.

John was very ill. There could be no doubt about that. Every breath was agony to him; yet the fever ran so high that, while his mind wandered, he tried to talk and sing, and even to spring out of his bed. He was quieter with his father's arms round him than in any other position, and for the greater part of the night Gideon sat holding him thus, while Obed, refusing to go to bed, sat over the fire, ready at any moment to compound a hot drink, administer medicine, or go to the doctor, as might be required. Keziah had been sent to bed; they had no need for her.

It was about ten o'clock that she had knocked at the parlour door, and said in her gruff way:

"Is missis a-coming back to-night or not?"

Obed looked helplessly at Gideon.

"I don't think so," said Gideon. There was not a spark of feeling in his tone. His eyes were fixed upon John's face.

"Then I may as well go to bed," said Keziah, "unless you'd like me to sit up wi' John."

"No; let her go to bed," said Gideon to his uncle.

"If missis *should* come home, then," said the maid-of-all-work, "I reckon you'll let her in?"

"Yes," said Obed.

Then Keziah shut the door, and the old man went up to Gideon, and laid his hand on his nephew's shoulder. Gideon knew that the touch was meant for comfort.

"She won't come back," he said suddenly, raising his eyes, already haggard and bloodshot, to his uncle's face. "She's left me."

"Nay, nay, Gideon; she was fond of thee—fond o' the lad. She's made a mistake wi' trains, or summat, as the doctor said."

"The doctor's a fool," said Gideon. "What does it matter? There's the boy to think of; it's time for his medicine now."

And he spoke not another word, except to little John, until the morning hour.

"No better, I'm afraid," the doctor said, with a grave look, as he stood by the bedside on the early Sunday morning. "Hadn't you better have a nurse?"

"Do you mean," said Gideon, "that a woman could do more for him than we can?"

"I don't know that she would actually do more: she might think of things you wouldn't think of. Now, Gideon, don't be absurd. I'll just send Mrs. Worlaby in, and then——"

"I will have no Mrs. Worlaby in the house—

unless I am injuring the boy by refusing," he said, with an ominous frown upon his face. "But I think I can nurse him as well as any woman in the world. Look at him: he's quieter with me than with anyone else. I can do everything for him that is necessary."

"But you'll want your night's rest."

"Do you think I should take *rest* while he is like this?"

The doctor shrugged his shoulders, and recognised that there was something keener in Gideon's love for his child than that of most men for their offspring. He yielded the point.

"I don't say but what you'll do as well as a nurse, if you can spare the time and will take the trouble."

And then he launched into new directions, to which Gideon listened with eager attention. In his heart the doctor felt that no hired nurse would tend the child like Gideon; but he went away shaking his head.

"I doubt whether the boy will get over it," he said to himself; "and Gideon will take it hard. It will be all the worse for him if he nurses the child to the end. And what on earth has become of that vain little piece of wickedness, his wife?"

Nobody could answer that question. There was an eight o'clock post on Sunday morning, but no other until Monday. No telegram had arrived. A rumour of Emmy's disappearance roused her mother to desperate anxiety, and she consulted nervously with Mr. Blake as to the steps to be taken on Monday, if nothing were heard of her. The police were communicated with, for Mrs. Enderby firmly believed that her daughter had met with some frightful accident, which alone could account for her absence. Gideon did not seem anxious, or even, perhaps, concerned. He was wrapped up in the care of his boy. He was like a man stunned with one blow, who does not seem to feel the pain of a second. Consciousness would return by and by.

John was very ill. Through the long hours of the day, Gideon watched beside him, noting every change in the little face, where the crimson came and went as the child drew his painful, choking breaths; watched the progress of the disease, and fought it—ineffectually; for as time went on, it became very clear indeed that the childish strength was waning, and that the hours of the little life were drawing to a close.

Visitors came to the house in numbers, but were dismissed by Keziah, who had orders to admit nobody. Mrs. Blake came, but was politely conducted off the premises by Obed Pilcher, who made himself chief guard to the sick-chamber. John was to be kept quiet, the doctor said; and it was as much for Gideon's as for John's sake that Uncle Obed kept the door. To him it seemed as though Gideon were more like a wounded wild animal keeping savage watch over its young, than a mere human being. He listened to no word of comfort; he took neither food nor sleep; he never lifted his eyes from the dearly-loved little face, in which he had centred all his hopes and all his happiness—if not all his love. Obed would not let gaping observers in to see what was, to him, a strange and terrible sight.

The day crept to its height and sank again. Night came with its desolation, its weird horrors, its lurking possibilities of ill. The weather had changed during the afternoon, and the wind was getting up. It moaned restlessly round the house, whistling at every crevice, making door and window shake. Now and then a dash of rain was heard against the window-panes, and the swaying branches of rose-tree or jessamine tapped at the glass like an unearthly hand. More than once Obed fancied that he distinguished veritable finger-tapping; but he always sank back again in his chair, acknowledging the source of these strange noises, yet not without a gleam of superstitious doubt whether the sound he had heard might not have been "a call" for the dying child. He wondered if Gideon had heard. But Gideon, with his chin pillowed by his hands, and his elbows on his knees, saw nothing, heard nothing, but "the boy."

John was delirious that night. He was afraid of his own father—the father that loved him so—and beat him off with his little hands whenever Gideon came near. He wanted his mother, he said, and why did not mammy come?

"I do so want my mammy!" he wailed in his broken voice, with the pathetic, unseeing stare of his great eyes fixed reproachfully on Gideon. "Mammy would take the pain away; mammy would make John better."

It was piteous to hear; especially when the listeners reflected that his mother had shown so very little love for him. But there are few things that rend the heart more terribly than the wild words spoken in delirium by those we love, or an absence of recognition in the eyes of those for whom we would willingly lay down our lives.

Once Gideon lost his self-control, and cried out in remonstrance:

"John, John, don't you know me—your own father? Don't push me away, lad; I've done thee no harm."

"He doesn't know, Gideon," said old Obed, hobbling to his nephew's side—"he doesn't know."

"My God!" said Gideon, his reserve breaking down as it seldom broke down save in his old uncle's presence, "I don't know how to bear it—that he shouldn't know my voice!" And a dry sob shook his broad shoulders as he covered his face for one moment with his hands. "John—laddie," he said, raising himself again, "say one word to your daddy—say that you know him now."

But John pushed him away, and wailed bitterly for his mother.

Morning found him very weak. The delirium had died down, for the fever had left him; but he lay so still and white, with such purple shades about his eyelids and his lips, that more than once Obed almost thought him dead. Dr. Miller, who came very early, shook his head over his condition. He gave orders about nourishment and cordials, saying that the child's strength must be kept up as much as possible. And he would come in again and see how things went on.

The postman came as the doctor went out of the gate. It was the London post, and there was a letter for Gideon.

Obed Pilcher took it at once to his nephew, who was sitting in a sort of trance of absorbed anxiety at John's bedside. He looked very haggard, but the doctor had insisted on his swallowing food and hot coffee, and he was more composed than he had been during those dreary midnight hours. He looked at the letter which Obed put into his hand as if he did not know what to do with it.

"Open it, lad. It's from Emmy, belike."

Gideon turned away his face.

"Wunnot thee open it? She may say when she's a-comin' back."

At this appeal Gideon drew himself slowly up, and dragged the envelope open. It seemed an effort to him even to take his eyes from John's white face. He read the letter—it contained only a few lines—and let it drop from his fingers.

"I knew it," he said, in a dull undertone. Then he resumed his silent watch, with his eyes fixed on the boy. But his face had turned to an ashy whiteness, like that of Jacky's lips.

Obed picked up the letter and straightened it out between his shaking fingers.

"You can read it," Gideon muttered. And Obed read.

"When you get this letter," Emmy had written, "I shall be far away, and you need not look for me, for you will never find me, and I do not want to see you any more. I have found someone who loves me better than you ever did, and I have given up everything for his sake. You had better forget me as soon as you can—I dare say it won't be difficult. I hope you will always be kind to Jacky, and think no more of

"EMMY."

Obed Pilcher was parish-clerk, and felt himself a pillar of the church, but after reading this letter, it must be recorded that he swore. If his curse could have rested on Emmy's fair false head for ever, and weighed it down to everlasting woe, he would have gladly uttered it again.

"Hush!" said Gideon, looking up with haggard eyes. "The boy will hear."

"But bean't you going to do something, Gideon? To send after her—to punish the man, whoever 'tis——"

"Afterwards," Gideon answered quietly, and turned again to the boy. And Obed knew that he must say no more.

There were still some fluctuations in John's condition, and more than once the father's heart was thrilled with the belief that he was about to recover, after all, and then sank, heavy as lead, when an unfavourable symptom declared itself.

Joseph Blake and his wife were allowed to steal in gently in order to see the little boy. The parson called, but was not admitted; and a hundred inquiries were made at the door, and dismally answered by Keziah. Gideon had never been a favourite in the town, and Emmy had earned much disapproval for herself; but little John was one of those bright-faced children of whom everyone took friendly heed, and his comparatively recent escape from drowning had brought him into prominence. No sick child in the town received half so much attention as was just then bestowed on Jacky. But it brought no solace to his father's wounded heart.

It was in the early dawn of Tuesday morning that full consciousness came again to the child for a little while. He opened his dark eyes suddenly and smiled into his father's face. Gideon's heart throbbed so painfully that he could not speak, but he bent down and kissed the boy's forehead.

"I've been asleep," said John.

His voice was almost inaudible.

"Yes, my lad. Here, drink this; it will do you good."

12

John drank, and spoke in stronger tones.

" Where's mammy ? " he said.

A quiver passed over Gideon's face.

" She's away just now," he answered.

" Gone to heaven ? " said John, with the queer familiar speech of another world which seems so natural on childish lips.

An inspiration came to Gideon's mind. It would be better for John to think that his mother had died, and so he bowed his head.

" Oh ! " said the boy. Then, after a pause : " John's goin'—too."

He shut his pretty eyes as if he meant to sleep, and Gideon, with a hideous grip of pain at his heart, saw the death-damp gather on his brow.

It lasted an hour or two—that agony of dying. It seemed to Gideon cruel that a little child should bear such pain. But perhaps it was worse for Gideon to witness than for the child to bear. And at last old Obed laid the tiny waxen hands across each other and drew Gideon from his place.

" It's all over," he said sorrowfully. " Try to bear it, Gideon. He's gone."

Gideon rose from his knees, and looked from

the child's placid lifelessness into his uncle's rugged, wrinkled face, as if he scarcely understood what had been said. As Obed's hand still pressed his arm and drew him from the bed, he made two steps towards the middle of the room, and then fell, like a log, prone upon the floor at Uncle Obed's feet.

CHAPTER VII.

"Would it were I had been false, not you!"

"It's a great mystery," remarked Mrs. Blake, primly folding one black-gloved hand over the other.

"It is indeed a terrible dispensation," answered her friend, Miss Lethbury. "So young a child to be taken—and the mother left!"

Miss Lethbury was a spinster of profoundly Evangelical views and an acid temperament, both of which characteristics had endeared her to Mrs. Blake, who was not religious herself, but liked other people to be so—if, at least, they did not carry their religion to any inconvenient length. There was this advantage about Miss Lethbury: she never allowed her Evangelicalism to modify the sharpness of her criticism of her neighbours; on the contrary, it seemed sometimes to add an edge to it. She was straight and tall and spare; her long nose and straight upper lip gave her a look of severity which her words seldom belied.

She was sitting with Mrs. Blake till the mourning-carriage should arrive. Joseph Blake and his wife were to be present at little John's funeral that afternoon, and Miss Lethbury had dropped in, *en passant*, to hear the news. She would have ample time to walk to the cemetery afterwards, for the Blakes would have to be driven to Gideon's house before the final ceremony began.

"I always said that Emmy Enderby was very deep," said Mrs. Blake, lowering her tones. "It's a dreadful thing to have come upon the family. My husband's nearly heart-broken about it; and Carry she says she'll go away, she can't hold up her head in Casterby again."

"Yes, it's very bad for a girl's prospects when such a thing happens," said Miss Lethbury, in tones of deepest commiseration.

"I don't see as it need affect Carry, and that's what I told her," said Mrs. Blake with dignity. "It's no relation of hers, nor yet of her father's or mine. It's Enderbys as ought to feel it most, I think. But there, they were all of that light-minded sort, and I was not one bit surprised; but it has nothing to do with *us*."

"Well, perhaps you are right, Mrs. Blake," said Miss Lethbury. "But what will Mr. Gideon do? Is he going to get a divorce?"

"Nobody knows," answered Mrs. Blake, shaking her head dolorously. "He won't allow anybody to mention the matter to him. He was always so strange—so shut-up and reserved, you know. Scarcely anyone has seen him or spoken to him since the little boy's death. But I should think he would get a divorce: there could be no difficulty.

"It's quite Scriptural to divorce a woman like that," said Miss Lethbury. "And then he could marry some nice, quiet girl—Mary Tucker, for instance—and be happy. I suppose there's no doubt as to who it was she went off with?"

"Not the least. It was that Captain Hamilton that was once engaged to Miss Lisle. They were seen together at Retford. And they say Miss Lisle fainted when she heard that Emmy was gone. You may depend on it, *she* knew."

"She may thank her stars that she found out his wickedness before it was too late!"

"He'd broken it off before then," said Mrs. Blake. "Don't you remember that Friday afternoon at tea, when Emmy took up the cudgels for him, and cried afterwards? I thought there was something very queer about it then."

"Hard-hearted little minx!" said Miss Lethbury, indignantly. "I should like to whip her round the town for her behaviour! Depend on it, that's the way in which women of *her* sort should be treated."

"I shudder to think," Mrs. Blake responded in sepulchral tones, "that she sat at *my* table, and conversed with *my* friends and *my* child! Gideon was very much to blame for not restraining her more; but he is punished for it now."

"I trust that the judgments of God may be blessed to his soul."

"Well, I don't know," said Mrs. Blake, doubtfully; "Gideon never set up to be religious, and I haven't heard that there's been any change in him. He wouldn't see Mr. Fletcher, nor his curate neither, when they called. And,

mercy me! there's the carriage. Well, good-bye,
Lydia. We shall see you, maybe, at the cemetery."

"I'm going to walk down there now," said
Miss Lethbury. "There'll be a good crowd o'
folk. They want to see how Gideon takes it."

"Ay, there's been a deal of talk about Gideon," said Mrs. Blake, dismally. And then she
joined her husband in the passage, put her black
kid hand into his arm, and walked ceremoniously
down the garden-path with him to the mourning-carriage at the door.

Such ceremony was befitting to the occasion;
for, as Gideon was in such desperate trouble,
the Blake family and their friends thought to
comfort him by honouring his boy's funeral.
The action was meant in kindness; but I do not
think that Gideon drew any consolation out of
it. In fact, the crowd of people, relations and
others, worried him whenever it forced itself upon
his consciousness.

As Mrs. Blake had said, scarcely anyone had
seen him since the day of John's death. He
had shut himself up in his own room, or in the

room where the child's dead body lay, and exchanged words with no one save Obed Pilcher. As to his work, that seemed to be completely forgotten; but his father, who was extremely distressed on his account, sent word to him not to come back to the yard until he felt inclined. Obed gave the message, but it was doubtful whether Gideon heard it. If his father had not given him his freedom just then, he would have taken it. He was beyond the binding of laws.

Old Obed managed all the details of the child's funeral. He felt that it would not do to trouble Gideon with them. Even to him Gideon did not speak. He seemed possessed by a dumb devil; he scarcely ate; and he slept very little—Obed could hear him pacing the floor of his room for hours at a time—and in the sight of others, at least, he did not shed a tear. But when the little coffin-lid had been finally shut down, Obed stood outside the parlour-door listening to the storm of sobs which shook the father's frame from head to foot, as he knelt beside the coffin with his head upon the lid. Every sob seemed to pierce Obed's heart with almost as sharp a pang as those which Gideon endured; but the old man, too feeble now to be able to indulge his grief in this passionate way, turned away from the door with shaking hands and head, and, going into the kitchen, sent Keziah out of the house upon some trivial errand, so that she should not hear and gossip about those terrible, gasping sobs.

Gideon was hardly conscious at this time of the silent, wakeful love of the old man, which encompassed, and shielded him at every turn. But Uncle Obed was the only person whom he could bear to see, and he leaned upon him without knowing it.

Obed Pilcher had not much imagination, but such as he had made him nervous concerning the funeral. He would have been glad if Gideon could have been kept away from it, and thought that it would almost be an advantage if he were taken ill. Dr. Miller prognosticated an illness, and told the old man to be on the watch for symptoms. But Gideon was apparently well, although he looked white and haggard. His strength would bear a good deal of strain, and there were no signs as yet of its giving way.

Even on the day itself, when he insisted on carrying the child's coffin on his knees in the mourning-carriage, he seemed perfectly composed. His face was like a mask—rigid, expressionless; but for its almost deadly pallor it had not changed. He went through the ceremony with the same appearance of calm; and even the presence of a crowd, and the curious though not entirely unsympathetic stare of his townsfolk, did not disconcert him. Possibly he did not even know that they were there.

It was not then so much the custom as it is now to place flowers about the dead; but on this occasion a great wreath of white blossoms was laid upon the little coffin just before it was lowered into the grave. Gideon, looking down upon it, never noticed who placed it there. Not till long afterwards was he told that the flowers had been sent by Frances Lisle. She had reason—poor Frances!— to be sorry for herself; but she could spare a crumb of sorrow from her loaf for Gideon Blake and his child.

"He looked pretty much as usual," said Miss Lethbury afterwards. "Not a tear nor nothing.

Old Obed Pilcher was a sight to see, with the tears running down into his wrinkles, and sobbing when he ought to have made the responses; and all the rest of the family, with white handkerchiefs at their eyes. But Gideon stood there, his arms straight down by his sides, and his eyes on the grave, just for all the world as if he didn't care."

She did not understand the only signs of sorrow that Gideon knew how to make. His father, standing beside him, knew better. He saw how "the lad," as he tenderly called him, swayed at one moment, as if he would have fallen. He noted the dazed look in his eyes when the last words of the funeral service had been read; and he whispered an emphatic warning to Obed as they returned to the carriages at the cemetery gate.

"See after the lad," he said, "or he'll be off his head before long, poor chap!"

And Obed nodded assent.

When all the rites were over, and the friends departed from the desolate house, Obed ventured timidly upstairs to the room whither Gideon had betaken himself, with a strange fear at his heart. But Gideon was neither sobbing nor raving, nor had he cut his throat—which were the things which haunted old Obed as possibilities night and day; he was simply standing by a chest of drawers, with a black bag in his hand.

"What art doing, Gideon?" said Obed, startled from his intention of saying a comforting word.

"Packing," said Gideon.

He rammed some articles hastily into the bag as he spoke.

"Packing, lad? And for what?"

"I am going to London," said Gideon, after a moment's pause.

It seemed as though he had hesitated whether to answer the question or not.

Obed uttered a great cry.

"Nay, lad, nay! *Not* to London—*not* to seek out those who have sinned, and make 'em suffer for their sin. Leave vengeance to God."

"You're a good man, Uncle Obed," said Gideon, with terrible gentleness, "and I know you mean well; but you don't understand."

"I'll prevent thee!" panted Obed, laying his shrivelled hands on his nephew's arm, as though he could detain him by main force. "I'll not let thee go. I'll put the police on thee. She isn't worth it. Gideon—the jade's not worth it. Thee shall never hang for that little slut, Emmy Enderby."

Gideon looked very dark for a moment or two; then his brow cleared, and he put his uncle's hand away from him with a wan smile.

"You're mistaken, Uncle Obed," he said quietly. "I've no intention of hanging for her, nor for anyone. I'm going to London on my own business, and you can't prevent me."

"I'll swear the peace on thee. Thou bean't fit to leave Casterby," said Obed in haste.

"You'll do nothing at all," said Gideon, with a touch of the old imperiousness in his tone. "I shall go my own gait, and you'll leave me to it. Else you and I will have words, and part company, maybe."

It was a threat which reduced poor old Obed to instant submission. He could bear anything but dissension between Gideon and himself. He resorted to entreaty instead of denunciation.

"Thee wean't get thyself into trouble, Gideon? Tha'rt all I've got left i' this world. Thee'll come back safe and sound?"

"Ay, I'll come back," said Gideon, with mechanical assent, and he went on packing the things into his bag, then shut it with a snap.

"Thee wean't be able to find her," quavered Obed, in a lower tone.

But Gideon only gave him a look in return. He was not going to betray his plans and purposes; his mouth was shut fast—firm as marble. Obed sighed and was silent. He saw Gideon grasp his bag and go downstairs; he followed him groaning.

"Ah'll go wi' thee to t' station," he said.

"As you like," Gideon answered, in an abstracted tone.

The two men left the house and struck into the meadows, by which route they could avoid the highroad for some little distance. Neither of them spoke. They did not walk fast, but Obed groaned occasionally as though he were exhausted; perhaps he had a faint idea of making Gideon lose the train. If this were so, Gideon divined his purpose, for he stopped short in the middle of a field and faced his uncle resolutely.

"This will do," he said. "We'll say good-bye

here, Uncle Obed. I shall be late if I walk at this pace."

" When wilt be back, lad?"

" Good-bye, Uncle Obed."

" Lad, thee'll come back to me? For pity's sake, doan't leave me to die here alone, Gideon. I loved the little lad, too."

Gideon wrung his uncle's hand; perhaps it was impossible for him to speak. At any rate, he made no answer, but turned his back on old Obed Pilcher, and swung off hurriedly to the station. Obed stood watching him, until the haze of distance and of approaching twilight hid him from view. Then the old man, looking ten years older, and more shaken than he had ever looked before, crept back to his desolate home.

Gideon gave no account of the next two days to any man. It would have been almost out of his power to do so. There remained in his memory only vague impressions of maddening gloom, of strange faces, of lighted streets and empty squares, of bewilderment unutterable, and a burning desire of revenge upon the man who had in-

jured him. He could not have told afterwards
what he did with himself all day long. He slept
at a quiet little hotel, the name of which he had
learnt from his father, who had stayed there once
or twice in his life; and in the daytime he wandered about the streets, haunted the Park, looked
up at windows, vaguely hoping to see Emmy's face
at one of them. London in itself produced no
impression upon him. Endless rows of houses,
crowded pavements, a throng of strangers amongst
whom he was for ever seeking the face that he
knew—this was all that London meant for him.

He had by some chance heard that Captain
Hamilton had rooms near Bond Street. The clue
was small enough, but it had been sufficient to send
him to London and to cause him to haunt the
West End. Probably neither Emmy nor Captain
Hamilton knew that he had even this ghost of a
clue. And, moreover, it was very unlikely that
Gideon Blake would come across them, for Hamilton had made up his mind to take his companion
first to Paris, and then to the South of France,
so as to be out of the way of any "unpleasantness."

13

Hitherto he considered that he had escaped "unpleasantness" very fairly. He had managed to quarrel with Frances and break off that engagement before eloping with Mrs. Gideon Blake, with whom he considered himself quite romantically in love. In fact, he had lost his head over Emmy, he said to himself. And, after all, she was a mere nobody—a lout of a carpenter's wife—and she would have gone off with somebody else, if not with him; he was quite sure of that. She was of that *pâte;* she was not the woman to keep straight, and he might as well profit by her weaknesses as any other man. That was the way in which George Hamilton thought of Emmy. And he was responsible to nobody; he had no relations to speak of, and if he chose to enjoy himself, why should anyone object?

The nuisance was that Emmy had no decent clothes. She wanted doing up all round. She had no boots, or gloves, or ribbons, let alone dresses and hats, that Captain Hamilton could walk out with. She must get herself a few things in London, he told her, and she should have a complete rig-out when they got to Paris.

He was sorry afterwards that he had delayed even for those few days in London. Emmy left her home on the Saturday night, and John (although Emmy did not know it) died on Tuesday; the funeral took place on the following Saturday afternoon. Captain Hamilton and Mrs. Hamilton, as he called her, meant to leave England on the next Tuesday. Emmy had wanted a new frock, and could not get it before Monday. She said that she was obliged to stay, and Captain Hamilton lessened the risk of being tracked by staying at a big hotel on the Embankment, instead of going to his old rooms in Ebury Street.

It was a hundred to one against their being seen by Gideon—the unsophisticated countryman to whom all London streets were equally puzzlingly alike—even if he came to London in search of his missing wife. But it is the unlikely thing that happens. Hamilton took Emmy out for a drive on Monday afternoon, and as they were driving back to the hotel Gideon saw them from the pavement.

They did not see him. Emmy was smiling and lovely, with a picturesque gray hat and feathers shading her exquisite little face, and a gray dress trimmed with soft gray fur, for the weather was growing cold enough for warm stuffs and trimmings. She looked far prettier in gray than in the blues and pinks with which she used to be so fond of bedizening herself. Gideon saw her plainly for one moment—saw, also, the evil, cruel face beside her—and then the carriage had passed him, and he had lost—or nearly lost—his chance.

He made a wild spring forward. He wanted to stop the horses, or to throw himself over the carriage door and drag the villain from his place; but his attempt was, of course, an utter failure. One or two men dragged him back, swearing at him for his temerity; they thought he was only a country bumpkin trying to cross the road. Gideon shook them off, and set off to run, keeping the carriage steadily in sight. The horses were going slowly, and that was in his favour; also they were at no great distance from the hotel. Gideon stopped short and watched as they left the carriage and entered the big portico. Now that he could have confronted them, could have forced them to speak to him, he drew back, cold, sick, trembling, almost afraid. It would be easy to face *him*, but he could not bear to look Emmy in the face. He was ashamed for her—he would not cover her with shame and confusion before all the people who stood by. He would spare her that punishment, and never look upon her face again. But he meant to punish Hamilton.

His desperation gave him cunning and courage. He hung about the building, and made friends with a commissionaire, who in turn introduced him to the boots when he came out with some luggage. Gideon soon learned that Captain and Mrs. Hamilton were staying in the house, but leaving for Paris on the morrow. The Captain generally went out for a stroll after dinner with a cigar. " Not a bad place for a stroll," said Boots, indicating the Embankment with a nod and a grin. Gideon gave them some money to get rid of them when he had found out all that he wanted to know. Then he set himself to wait, within sight of the door, for his enemy.

The daylight changed into gloom, and then into the glare of dim yellow light which came from the gas-lamps. The roar of the street surged around

Gideon until it almost stupefied him. Cabs whirled by; heavy omnibuses and vans lumbered slowly along; a man with a truck of fruit bawled his wares continuously in his ear. Gideon stood in a recess where he could see the people who came out and in. Visitors arrived with cabs laden with luggage; later on these arrivals became infrequent. There was a perpetual whistle for cabs from a stand over the way; and then ladies and gentlemen in evening dress would come out of the big portico and drive away. Gideon became very much afraid lest the man he sought should escape him in this way. Not that he should not recognise him in evening dress, but that if Emmy was at his side Gideon feared that his strength would fail.

But about ten o'clock, when Gideon had almost begun to despair, the man he sought came out of the hotel. He paused at the door to light his cigar, and in the glare of the lamps, Gideon noted every feature of the cold yet sensual face of his wife's betrayer. George Hamilton was in his way a handsome man, but he had always been a very self-indulgent one; he had never denied himself a pleasure that he could procure at any cost, in his life, and thirty years of unbridled and often vicious habits had left their imprint on the lines of his face. These were a little more apparent than usual when Gideon stood looking at him ; for he was not on his good behaviour, and he must have known in his heart that he had done a peculiarly mean thing.

Gideon did not theorize, he did not even say to himself that Hamilton's face was bad ; but he knew that he hated it with a vindictive hatred which made him long to see it lying in the dust at his feet. It was not in his mind to kill the man. He wanted rather to make him suffer, to see him writhe with pain and cry for mercy—to disgrace him in the world's eyes and in his own. Life and death were not the issues in his mind just then, although he was hardly concerned as to whether Hamilton lived or died.

Captain Hamilton lighted his cigar, and turned towards the Embankment, where he liked to take a short walk between dinner and bedtime. He had given up the slight nervous fear of meeting Gideon Blake which he had felt at first. Emmy had so impressed him with Gideon's ignorance and stupidity that he did not think the young man capable of finding him out.

There were not many people on the Embankment, but it seemed to Gideon that the broad sidewalk was inconveniently full. At last he quickened his pace, and touched Captain Hamilton on the shoulder. Hamilton turned with a start.

" I want to speak to you," said Gideon.

Captain Hamilton's face turned white. He looked round for help; but no policeman was in sight, and for the moment the street looked deserted. They were near a flight of steps leading down to one of the piers, and Gideon edged him steadily towards the wide square landing or bay at the head of the steps, where they were comparatively secure from observation. It need scarcely be said that George Hamilton did not like this movement on Gideon's part.

" I don't know you," he said, trying to pass him, and feigning non-recognition. " I have nothing to say to you. I——"

" I said I had something to say to *you*," remarked Gideon quietly. " You know who I am very well. My wife is with you now at that hotel.

No, you needn't call out; I'll throw you over the parapet if you do. I came to London to tell you that you are a damned villain, and to give you— *this!*"

It was a blow which felled Hamilton to the ground. He did not even cry out; Gideon waited a moment, raised his fist to strike again, then let it drop to his side. He could not strike a man who did not resist. He was not a savage; he was an Englishman who believed in a fair fight, not in murder. If Hamilton had moved or cried out, Gideon would not have spared him. But a shapeless, motionless heap on the wet ground at his feet, what could he do to that?

"Get up," he said, touching him contemptuously with his foot—"get up and take the rest of it. I'll break every bone in your body before I've done with you."

The fierceness was rising within him; although his voice was still low, it had a savage tone. He threw himself down, and turned the man round roughly, to see whether he had fainted or not. But Hamilton's face was more ghastly than any that Gideon had ever seen. It wore a strangely livid hue, and the blood that had trickled from a wound upon his temple was already black and coagulated. The pinched look of the nose and mouth brought back to Gideon's mind a picture of the dead body of his little child. So John had looked before they laid him in the grave.

It was not that he renounced or regretted his plans of vengeance when he saw Hamilton lying thus before him, with the pallor of the grave upon his face. It was only that this remembrance of John's white baby brow and sunken eyes, with their darkened lids, made him giddy and confused. He hardly knew what he had done or what he meant to do. Nobody had noticed the encounter; nobody in passing seemed to see the dark heap with the up-turned white face upon the paved space at the head of the steps. Gideon turned his back upon it, and walked away. His mind was dazed, and he did not think of calling for help or of ascertaining Hamilton's condition more precisely. He left the steps, and walked towards the City, not knowing whither he went or what he did.

At midnight he found himself on a seat in one of the embrasures of a great stone bridge. He knew that it was midnight, because he heard the deep tones of a great bell sending its reverberations far and wide over the shimmering waters and the silent City streets. It was this sound which had roused him from the stupor into which he had fallen. He looked round him, and did not know where he was. It might have been another world, for anything he could tell. He had not seen anything like it in his life before. Below the bridge, and for some distance, he saw the dark and sullen water, studded with black shapes here and there— barges with lamps fixed to their prows, of which the ripples sent back a quivering reflection. Far away in the distance other lights could be seen— long rows of them in threes on either side the bank, and points of single radiance, red and white and green, at intervals. At one side a dim dome-like building broke the horizontal lines of roofs and banks. It was the bell of St. Paul's that Gideon had heard. Above the river there was a cloudy sky, with no light of moon or stars; but the night was fairly warm, although Gideon shivered where he sat.

All the past broke upon him suddenly. He remembered the years of his married life—years of disappointment, sweetened only by the love and hope which John had brought into it—he remembered John's death and Emmy's desertion, and his own revenge. He looked down at his hand in dull amaze. "I am a murderer!" he said to himself. He thought of the stir that would be made in Casterby when news came that he, Gideon Blake, was in prison for killing George Hamilton. Well, all who knew him would say that he was right. Only there would be the disgrace of prison, the punishment—for he did not doubt that he would be hanged—and the broken lives and hopes that would follow in its train. For the Casterby folk would never let the Blakes forget that one of their family had been hanged. They would have to leave the place where they had lived so long and been thought so well of. And Obed—old Obed—he would die of a broken heart.

Was there any way out of it?

He looked over the parapet, and saw the dark waters glancing underneath. If he threw himself into the river and was drowned, would not everybody be thankful? Then there would be no exposure, no disgrace. Hamilton would be dead; Gideon would have disappeared, and there was an end. Emmy was nothing to him now. He could not believe that she had any claim upon him; he shrank even from thinking of her. She must go to the workhouse, or beg her bread from door to door, he supposed; he did not know what became of women like her. She could but fall to lower depths; he, too, would fall lower if he lived—he the murderer, and she the harlot!

He shivered violently, and raised his head to look round. There was no one in sight. The policeman who had eyed him curiously two or three times was quite at the other end of the bridge. He lifted himself cautiously, and put his hands on the parapet, dragging his legs up on the stone coping so as to be ready for a spring. He knew that he must be swift, or he would be observed and stopped. He began to draw himself up into the necessary posture, when suddenly a strong hand seized his arm and pulled him back.

"That's a dangerous amusement," said a young strong voice. "What do you mean by it?"

VIII.

" Because I seek Thee not, oh, seek Thou me !
Because my lips are dumb, oh, hear the cry
I do not utter as Thou passest by,
And from my life-long bondage set me free ! "

GIDEON struggled for a moment, then suc-
cumbed. The hands that held him were stronger
than his own. He broke out in wild appeal.

" Let me go ! " he said. " For God's sake, let
me go ! There's no place for me in this world. It
would be the truest kindness to let me get out
of it."

" Why should you go to another world where
there is also no place for you ? " said the stranger.

He was not much older than Gideon himself,
and far less robust-looking ; but he had an alertness
of glance, a resoluteness of manner, which ac-
counted for Gideon's submission. He was subdued
by the moral power of the man, not by his physical
strength.

"I don't care where I go," Gideon answered, again striving to break away. "I've come to the end of everything."

"Even to the end of God's mercies?" said the other man.

Gideon uttered a fierce word of blasphemy.

"I've lost everything I care for in the world," he went on. "My boy's dead; my wife has left me; I've just killed the scoundrel that enticed her away; I shall be hanged for it if I give myself up. Don't you think I should be better dead?"

"No, indeed I don't," said the new-comer. "I should say you were about the last person that ought to die, and you're coming home with me."

"I—I come home with you? I can't," said Gideon; but as he spoke he turned faint, and the whole world swam before his eyes.

He staggered, and the other man, slighter and shorter although he was, seized him by the arm and obliged him to lean upon him until they got off the bridge.

Gideon dimly remembered being helped into a cab, and then for a time he knew no more.

He had a narrow escape of brain-fever. For

several days he lay in a strange, semi-comatose condition, unable to speak or think, and suffering frightful pain in the head, alleviated only by constant applications of ice. He was thankful, in a vague way, for the relief which was afforded him; but he was not strong enough to ask whether he was in a hospital or a workhouse, or among friends. What friends, indeed, had he to nurse him? He had not the energy to ask questions. He was only too thankful to lie still, and to feel the throbbing of his head become gradually less, in a darkened chamber, with soft, cool bandages upon his aching brow.

Little by little he came to recognise his most constant nurse and visitor as the young man who had saved him from committing suicide from Black-friars Bridge. This young man wore in the house a narrow black gown, which Gideon was not learned enough to call a cassock, and almost any eye but that of an inexperienced country lad would have recognised the fact that he was of the priestly profession. There was a look, a manner, that was unmistakable; but the gracious kindliness of the one, the somewhat ascetic refinement of the other, were, to Gideon, simply individual traits, and therefore the more fascinating.

When he was well enough to consider the matter, Gideon contemplated the young priest with a curious mingling of sensations. Here was a man of his own age or thereabouts, whose whole life, as Gideon vaguely felt, was led upon principles so utterly different from his own that they almost alarmed and repelled him. There was an attraction about them too—or about the man, Gideon could not say which it was. He led a life of entire self-abnegation: so much was clear. The room in which Gideon lay was Father John's own room—the young priest was styled Father John by everybody, and Gideon never inquired about his other name— and a bare, white-washed little room it was. Gideon had Father John's bed, and the priest slept contentedly on the floor. The sick man used to watch his host sometimes when he was thought to be asleep; and nothing in his life ever amazed him more than Father John's prayers at night and morning before the black and white crucifix that hung upon the ugly white wall. Sometimes they were in Latin, and then Gideon went to sleep; but when

14

they were in English, and said aloud, Gideon would listen as if he were in a wonderful dream. For it was to him like a dream, that a man should kneel down and talk to some unseen Power, and ask, not only for grace and help in general terms, but for individual gifts for individual persons, Gideon included, although the priest did not know him yet by name.

"This man that I have brought home," said Father John, in his specializing, half-familiar way —"this man with the load of trouble on his breast, Thou, Lord, knowest how to help him better than I can do; forget him not, O Lord, nor his sad and heavy burthen which weighs him down to the very earth with shame and pain and bitterness——"

"How do you know?" said Gideon from his bed.

Father John was on his feet in a moment, looking startled; but only for a moment.

"My dear fellow," he said in his ordinary tones, as he walked to the bed and re-arranged Gideon's tumbled coverings, "I thought you were fast asleep."

"I was wide awake, and I heard every word

you said. How do you know anything about me?"

"Don't you remember what you said to me on the night when I met you first?"

"I was on the bridge," said Gideon slowly. "I tried to jump into the river. You pulled me back. But I don't know what I said."

"You said—— Shall I tell you?"

"Yes, tell me," said Gideon, turning away his head.

"That you had lost your boy—your own child, was it? Ah, yes! And that someone else—your wife—had left you. Perhaps all this was a dream?"

"No," Gideon answered in a harder voice; "it was not a dream. And I killed the man—that's all. I suppose I told you that?"

"Yes, you told me that."

There was a little silence, and then Father John said, with great sweetness and gentleness of tone:

"God help you, my friend."

"It's too late," said Gideon gruffly.

"How can it be too late? God's mercies are infinite."

"Ay, that's all very well," Gideon said, trying to explain himself; "but what I mean is, that what's done is done, and I shall never be clear from it again."

"Clear from the feeling of guilt—the stain of wrong-doing?"

"I don't know. I can't get rid of that man's face—on the Embankment. He had been alive a minute before. . . . He had done me a great wrong, but—all the same, it's terrible to take a man's life." Gideon's voice sank to a sort of moan. "If there's anything true in—in—your religion and all that," he went on, "it means, I suppose, that I shall never see my boy again?"

Father John was silent for a moment.

"Was that on the night I met you?" he asked.

"Yes."

"I don't remember hearing of any case of the kind—any mysterious death on the Embankment. Can you tell me where it happened?"

Gideon tried to describe the place. He told the name of the hotel at which Captain Hamilton had been staying, and he told his enemy's name; but he did not tell his own.

"Will you let me make some inquiries?" said the kindly young priest. "I have an idea that he may, perhaps, only have fainted. I will find out without saying anything about you."

Gideon assented hopelessly. He was perfectly sure that Hamilton was dead.

The next day Father John came to his bedside, and smiled at him, then grew grave again and began to speak.

"God has been very good to you," he said; "He did not allow you to take your enemy's life. Captain Hamilton has been very ill, but he is out of danger now."

"Living?" said Gideon, starting up and then falling back again. "He is alive?"

"Yes, he is alive. He was found soon after you left him, and carried to a hospital."

"Is—*she*—with him?"

"I cannot tell you."

Gideon averted his head.

At first the priest thought that his communication had produced very little effect; but presently he found that his patient was weeping. A great sob shook his gaunt shoulders now and then. The

relief was almost more than he could bear. He had
hated George Hamilton, but it was an awful thing
to feel himself a murderer. Little by little he
dropped out words and sentences that told the
priest what he had felt.

"It isn't that I've been afraid of punishment for
myself; but it's the thought of one's father and
one's friends. . . . Every night I've fancied myself
in the dock, with the judge putting on his black
cap, and my father and Uncle Obed sitting on the
seats listening to hear him say 'hanged by the neck
till you are dead.' . . . And then, after that . . .
'Thou shalt not kill.' And my boy—I used to think
I saw him looking down at me, and asking if I were
a murderer . . . and stretching out his arms—in
vain."

"You wish to see him again?"

"I'd go through hell to see him again!" cried
Gideon, with a vehemence at which Father John
involuntarily raised a protesting hand.

But he saw that the young man meant no harm
by it. His love for John was a weapon which the
good priest laid hold of immediately for the good
of Gideon's soul.

It was no wonder that he expected to make a convert. But the time was not ripe for the discussion of ecclesiastical or theological points.

Here was a soul in pain; a heart rent and broke; a whole nature laid waste with passion and sorrow. What was there for Father John to do, but to speak of the comfort that faith can give, and the love of Father and Son for suffering humanity? It was the first time that Gideon had listened to religious teaching since he was a boy. And there was a strange revelation to him of love and sympathy in the exposition of One who suffered all things for the sake of man, and met with cruelty and treachery in return. He caught his breath as he heard—was it not really for the first time?—of "that stupendous life and death," of all that earth shuddered at and heaven grew black in witnessing. What did it mean for him—that supreme act of abnegation and of pity?

The priest awoke in the night to see the man he had saved from suicide kneeling at the foot of the crucifix, outlined blackly on the whitewashed wall, and to hear the sobs that shook him like a reed. He was wise enough to say nothing and lie still.

"God will speak to him," said the good priest to himself, controlling the hot impatience to *help* which tingled in his veins. "My words may do more harm than good. God will teach him in His own way."

And so perhaps He did; but it was not in the way that Father John expected.

Gideon was up and dressed next day; he was very quiet, almost apathetic in manner, and seemed scarcely to understand what was said to him by the little community of Catholic priests who had taken him in. They were very good to him. Between themselves, they speculated a little as to his name and station, and hinted to Father John that he should be brought to confession; but Father John shook his head and told them to give him time. Of course he was a heretic; but a heretic with a curious gift (so Father John thought) of assimilating what he was taught, even although he might have an equally curious incapacity for expressing it. He sat in the chapel sometimes with a look of entire absorption on his face, turned to the big crucifix that hung over the altar. "It seems as if I had been here before," he said once, when Father John spoke to him about his liking for the chapel. And the priest wondered whether the stranger might not some day take up his lot with them and change from carpenter to monk.

But one day Gideon strolled in the walled garden which lay at the back of the house, and heard the voices of children at play in the adjoining playground. The Fathers had a school and an orphanage, but Gideon had not as yet come across any of the pupils. He was very weak after his illness, which had been short but sharp; and although the priests allowed him to wander about the house and grounds at will, he had taken but little notice of the arrangements of the place. Now, for the first time, the tuneful laughter of children's voices struck upon his ear. He looked for a gate, found it, and stood in the playground, gazing spell-bound at the noisy, merry groups. These were the younger boys—little fellows from four to eight or ten years of age; and there was one with golden hair and dark eyes, who recalled vividly to Gideon's mind the image of the boy whom he had lost. Gideon felt no disposition, however, to speak to the child. He only looked and looked, with a wealth of longing in his hungry eyes. And when the children had gone back to school, he sat down on a bench and thought.

He thought of Casterby. For the first time he remembered that his father and his uncle did not know what had become of him. He thought of his father's steady affection for him, of Uncle Obed's absorption in him and his boy. What was the old man doing without him now? His father had a wife and children, but Obed had nobody. And for the first time it came home dimly enough to Gideon that Obed had loved him as he had loved John—with the same blind, adoring love, and that he, Gideon, had made very little return for that affection. He had been friendlier with his uncle than with anybody else; but he had never shown what he felt, it had not been his way. And perhaps Uncle Obed was enduring a share of the passionate yearning for a beloved face which Gideon himself bore when he thought of his dead son—the child who had gone to a far-away heaven whither the father sometimes thought that he should "never win."

He felt in his pocket for his purse. It was

there intact, and still contained three pounds in gold and some silver. He laid it out before him and considered what he would do with it.

He must get away. He must go back to Casterby. So much was clear to his still confused and beclouded mind. He had no wife, no child; but he had his father and his uncle to see. It was not his love for them that drew him home again, but the consciousness of his love for John. Also he wanted to see John's grave.

For the mode of his departure, I feel that excuses must be offered. He left the priests who had been so good to him without saying farewell. The fact was that his mind was not clear enough for a true appreciation of their kindness and their claims on his gratitude. And when, months afterwards, he came, as it were, more to himself, he was amazed and horrified to find that he did not know the name of the community nor the part of London in which it was situated. Probably it was near Hammersmith, for his memories of trees and gardens, and the vicinity of the river, pointed in that direction; but he was never sure. And the Fathers had scarcely known his name, nor the place whence he came nor his circumstances, and had no means of tracing him if they had wished to do so.

Before he went he separated two sovereigns and a half from his little hoard, and wrapped them in a piece of paper on which he wrote a few words to Father John. "I am obliged to go home," he wrote. "I thank you very much for your kindness to me. Perhaps you can use the enclosed for some of the poor people you know. I am going back to my own people." The letter was simply signed by his initials and addressed to Father John. He left it with the porter and walked away along the road which he had been told would lead to the heart of London. He inquired his way to the railway-station and took the next train to Casterby—all in the same common-place, spiritless way, and as if nobody in the world would be surprised at anything he had done.

Father John read the letter and grieved over it. He thought that he had not done enough for the spiritual benefit of his protégé. It was the nature of the man to blame himself, and not Gideon, against whom some of the other inmates of the house were moved to considerable wrath. "He might have told us something about himself instead of walking off in this way," they said between themselves. But Father John lay all night long before the altar, praying for the conversion of Gideon's soul, and for the forgiveness of that failure, that weakness on his own part, which had caused him to let the stranger's soul escape. "The blame is mine," said the young priest sadly, as he went about his work next day and for many days thereafter. And he prayed that another chance might be given him—another day or hour in which he might plead with Gideon to give himself utterly and entirely to a better life. . . . But he never saw Gideon again.

It seemed very strange to him to get out at the well-known little country station, and to walk down the road, with its green bordering of grass, to the High Street and the Market Place. The town struck him as dwarfed and stunted. But it was not looking its best on that November evening, with a mist rising from the river and a small drizzling rain steadily falling from the clouds. Everything looked damp and mildewed and desolate. It was six weeks since Gideon went away.

He did not go to his father's first of all. He thought more of Obed, perhaps, than of his father, and he went to Obed's cottage by the river. He did not meet anyone who recognised him on his way. As he turned down the lane he noticed that the river was very high, and that the meadows were half covered with water, and when he reached the garden-gate he saw that even the house had been assailed by the water. It was the one drawback to the houses by the river that they were sometimes visited by the floods, which were in wet autumns a source of danger, as they rose very rapidly and did considerable damage now and then. The garden-beds seemed to have been almost destroyed, and the water-mark was still visible on the walls of the house; but evidently the place had not been abandoned, for there was a light in one of the upper windows, and at sight of it Gideon's heart throbbed with a new feeling of affection and—almost—of joy.

He knocked at the door—knocked twice before any answer came. At last the upper window was opened a little way, and Obed Pilcher's gray head appeared.

"Who be ye down theer?" he asked.

"It's me — Gideon. Will you let me in, uncle?"

"*Gideon!*" The old man's voice rose to a shriek of joy. "Gideon! Lad! ah thowt thee mun be dead. Wait thee, lad, ah'm coming— doan't thee go away—ah've but to unbolt the door. Thee'll waäit? thee'll waäit?"

"Of course I'll wait, Uncle Obed," said Gideon, with a strange new gentleness of tone. "Don't hurry thyself."

But in another minute he heard the old man hobbling downstairs and fumbling—probably with trembling hands—at the bolts and locks of the door. When it was opened, and Gideon stepped inside, he found himself literally in his uncle's arms.

"Lad, lad! Ah thowt thee dead, but ah knew that if thee was above ground, thee'd come back to owd Uncle Obed."

"Did you think me dead, uncle?"

"Ay, that ah did, lad. And thou's bin at

death's door, too, as ah can see by tha faäce and eyes. Coom away in, an' ah'll get on my clothes and mak' up t' fire for tha: coom awaäy."

"Where's Keziah?" said Gideon, following his uncle to the kitchen.

"Gone, lad—gone. Ah didn't want no wimmin foalk about *me;* ah can fend an' fettle for mysel'."

"We'll see about that," said Gideon, with a touch of the old masterfulness, subdued, however, into a kindlier tone. "Go and get into your clothes, and leave the fire to me. Or get back to bed, and I'll come upstairs with you."

But his uncle would not agree to the latter proposition. Gideon was cold and wet, and must have something to eat and drink. So Gideon set to work to blow the embers of the fire into a blaze, and by the time old Obed came downstairs again in all the glory of his Sunday suit, there was a ruddy glow on the kitchen walls, and on the red-brick floor, with the rag carpet before the fender, and the kettle was already beginning to sing in a homelike, comfortable way. Gideon stood by the hearth, staring into the flames. The room might look cheery enough, but where were they gone who used to make the brightness of the house?

Uncle Obed came up and shook him by the hand. He had not much to say, but it relieved his feelings to work Gideon's arm up and down like a pump-handle. Then he suggested that his "lad" should go upstairs and change his wet clothes while tea was being made.

"Thee'll find all tha things as thee left 'em," he said.

Gideon said nothing, but went stolidly up to his own room. Obed bustled about the kitchen, setting out crockery and food; he heard Gideon's steps in the room above him at first, then he became aware that they had ceased. The meal was ready, but Gideon did not come, and all was silent overhead.

"Coom, Gid, supper's ready," said Obed, in a cheerful voice, as he stumped upstairs. But no answer came.

The door of the bedroom was wide open, and the candle was flaring, for Gideon had placed the tin candlestick down on the chest of drawers and left it in the draught. It was a pretty little room,

15

decorated in Emmy's taste with a good many pink ribbons and much white muslin; but it looked spotlessly clean and fresh. John's little empty cot stood between the big white-curtained bed and the wall. And Gideon had dropped down on his knees and hidden his face on the white counterpane of the bed, with his hands stretched out before him, clenched together—in prayer or agony?

"Lord forgi'e me," muttered Obed to himself. "And ah sent him up here all alone."

He stood within the doorway, not daring to speak or move, not knowing whether to stay or to go. Gideon was perfectly still; it was his motionlessness that struck terror to Obed's heart.

But after a time he stirred. He lifted his head, drew back his hands, and rose. There was a look on his face which Obed had never seen before— the expression of one whose renunciation is complete. In some vague fashion, Obed Pilcher knew from that moment that his nephew was an altered man.

"Is that you, Uncle Obed?" said Gideon, quite quietly. "I won't keep you waiting more than a moment. I'll come directly."

Then he turned to the chest of drawers and began to take out some clothes. He had not yet begun to change.

" I'll use Keziah's old room," he said.

And he betook himself to that small apartment immediately. Obed did not venture to protest. And in perfect silence Gideon next day removed all his belongings to the servant's former abode, and his uncle knew, as well as if he had been told in words, that the room which Emmy and John had occupied was to be left untouched, untenanted.

Gideon came down to supper with a grave, unmoved countenance, and spoke very little, but his manner to his uncle was, for him, curiously gentle. Obed poured out all the news of the town, but seduously refrained from asking questions, at any rate for a time. Questions came later, but the first thing was to make Gideon eat his supper.

" Is father well ? " said the young man, as they sat by the kitchen fire after supper.

Obed smoked a long clay; but Gideon, with his hands plunged in his pockets, had declined a pipe.

"Eh? Thou'st not seen him? Ay, he's middlin', but he's fretted above a bit about thee, Gideon."

"It's too late to go and see him to-night," said Gideon, looking up at the clock.

"Well, mebbe. He looks kind o' pined, thee'lt see. And wheer hast been, Gid, all this long while?"

"I've been in London," said Gideon, with his eyes fixed on the fire.

"Not—not—in prison, lad?" asked the old man tremulously, with one deep-veined old hand laid heavily on Gideon's arm.

"Prison? No," answered Gideon in astonishmen. "I've been ill, or I should have come home sooner. But why prison?"

"Ah thowt," said Uncle Obed in some confusion, "that they might ha' tooken thee there for threshin' that man. We heerd tell as he was found somewheers down by t' river with his head stove in, and though it didn't say i' th' paäper *who* did it, we all knew as it was thee."

"Ay, you were right," said Gideon heavily. Then came a long pause. "I well-nigh killed him," he continued at length in trembling tones. "I did my best. I should have been a murderer, Uncle Obed, if I'd succeeded. If I'd had blood upon my hand, would you have been so ready to take me in?"

"Ay, that I would, lad," cried the old man excitedly. "And would ha' shook the hand as did it, too. There's not a jury in the land as would convict thee for an act of justice like to that."

"You're a Christian, Uncle Obed; you go to church," said the young man inexorably. He had folded his arms on his breast, and his face was very stern and pale. "How can you tell me that it would be an act of justice to commit murder? Whatever it might be in a jury's eyes, you've got to consider what it would be in the eyes of—God."

He said the last words solemnly, the muscles in his cheek flinching as he did so, the only sign of effort that he showed. Obed sat amazed, staring at him.

"Lad," he said at last, almost letting his pipe slip to the ground in his astonishment, and speaking very slowly—"lad, hast got religion while thou'st been away?"

"I don't know," said Gideon. And then they sat in silence for a little while.

"Well, well!" exclaimed Uncle Obed at last, in a high-pitched, querulous voice, "it's the fust time i' my life as ah've bin towd ah was not a Christian. Ah've been clerk this fowty year, an' no one ever said *that* to me afore. An' all because ah spoke as the nat'ral man 'ud speak, ah taäkes it : because it seems a deal more proper that a man should foight the man as has maäde his wife a——"

"Stop that!" said Gideon fiercely. "I won't have her called names. As to the man—I did fight him, as you say, and well-nigh killed him : isn't that enough for you? Did you want to see me on the gallows first, and damned to hell afterwards?"

"Nay, nay, lad—nay. Doan't talk i' that fashion. Ah'm not such a domned fool as that coomes to. Thou'rt right eno'. Me parish clerk, an' preach murder? Why, no! An' I'm downright thankful to see thee back, saäfe an' sound ; an' thee mustn't mind an' owd man's tongue, Gideon, nor catch'n up so fast."

"I'm a fool myself, and a brute to say a hard word to you," said the young man starting up, with a flush on his face. " Forgive me, uncle. Don't think worse of me than you can help," he said, standing with one hand on his uncle's shoulder, so that the old man could not see his face. " I've had a good bit to bear, you know, and sometimes I've been almost beside myself — with — with trouble. Else, I shouldn't have stayed away so long. It was the thought of you, and—the boy, that brought me back. You shan't lose me—as I lost *him*."

The pauses between the words made them doubly significant. Obed Pilcher understood much more than Gideon could say. " God bless thee, lad, for coming back !" he said in a hoarse undertone.

" I'll not leave you again, uncle," said Gideon, in a firmer voice.

IX.

"Wer nie sein Brod mit Thränen ass——"

THE news of Gideon's return soon spread far
and wide. Between six and seven in the morning
he was back at the yard, beginning his usual day's
work. His father met him with a close clasp of
the hand and a long examining look, but he asked
no questions, and it was not until the two were
alone together, later in the day, that Gideon said an
explanatory word.

"I was ill in London. I wish I had written,
but everything seemed to go out of my head. I
never thought of it."

Joseph Blake nodded. He was looking worn
and gray, but he had not the heart to reproach
his son.

"Did you see—her?" he asked in a low voice.

"Once," said Gideon, turning away his face.

The father asked no more questions. He, too,

had heard of the mysterious attack on Captain Hamilton in London, and believed that Gideon had been the assailant; but as Hamilton himself had refused to give information, and evidently wished it to be thought that he had simply been knocked on the head by a pickpocket, no public accusation had been made. Joseph Blake was the last man to ask Gideon painful or unnecessary questions, and he tried to shut the mouths of his wife and daughter, but could not succeed. Where he failed, however, Gideon succeeded by a sudden frown, a flash of his eyes, and a single word. It became understood in the family and in the town that Gideon was not to be questioned about his own private affairs.

What was he going to do next? the townspeople queried. They expected him to take to evil courses, now that his wife had left him and his child was dead. There was nothing, they said, to hold him back. He had always been a wild one at heart, and he would, no doubt, plunge headlong into excess and drink himself to death. "And there's every excuse for him," they said, with a pleased sense of assisting at a tragedy. It would round

off the story so completely, to be able to say that
"the poor young man never got over it, and died
of delirium tremens six months after his wife
eloped,"—so completely and artistically, indeed,
that Casterby waited with actual impatience to see
the final act begun.

But Gideon disappointed the Casterby people.
It might be true to say that "he never got over it"
—he never would get over it as long as he lived—
but he showed no signs of taking to strong drink in
consequence. On the contrary, it was rumoured
that he had become a teetotaler (which was not
true), and that he did not even smoke. He took up
his abode once more with Uncle Obed, and could
not be drawn from his lair by any attraction in the
way of tea-parties. He and Obed led a very se-
cluded life. No servant-girl replaced Keziah; the
two men lived alone, and Gideon did most of the
work in the early mornings or late at night. Obed
Pilcher was growing too rheumatic and infirm to
move about very much, and even spoke of relin-
quishing his duties as parish clerk. Gideon cooked
his meals for him, made the fires, chopped wood,
and scrubbed floors like a veritable slave. His step-

mother was scandalized at seeing him engaged in such menial work.

"It really isn't respectable; you should have a servant. It looks as if your own father didn't pay you properly," she declared.

"I'd sooner do it myself, if father doesn't mind," said Gideon in his deliberate way.

He was a great deal more deliberate than he used to be, and very silent—even with Uncle Obed. Only when they were alone in the evenings, and Obed was smoking, Gideon would reach down a book and read aloud in the loud, monotonous voice that Obed loved to hear.

The reading was of a serious turn. They had once tried a novel—one of Emmy's brightly-bound volumes from the parlour shelves—but neither of them could stand the love-making scenes. Obed growled and pronounced them rubbish; Gideon stopped one night in the middle of one, and put the book back in its place with a nauseated air. They fell back upon standard books of travel and history, which Gideon procured from the town library, and they read the Bible a good deal. It was quite a new book to Gideon. On some evenings he cared to read nothing else. Then the "Pilgrim's Progress," which he had kept so long unread, fascinated him completely. Old Obed knew it pretty well, and patronized it as the work of a man who did not belong to the Church; but it gained a new charm to him when he heard it from Gideon's lips.

In the daytime the young man did his work soberly and seriously, without smiles, but also without the sullenness with which he had formerly been credited. His fellow-workmen did not know what to make of him. He had never been hail-fellow-well-met with them, but he had been in many respects as other men: ready for a drink, for a jest, sometimes for a blow. Now all this was changed. He was almost always silent; he neither drank nor jested; and he worked as if he had no other interest in the world. What depths of feeling underlay the stern quietude of his demeanour, nobody guessed, unless it were Uncle Obed or his father, Joseph Blake.

After working-hours, he devoted himself entirely to Obed. But the old man was very frail, and never recovered from the shocks which little John's death, Emmy's flight, and Gideon's subsequent disappearance had inflicted upon him. When the cold and dreary winter was over, and the crocuses were just beginning to lift up their golden and purple heads in the garden, Uncle Obed failed rapidly, and before Easter was gone. He slipped away in his sleep while Gideon was reading to him one night from the Gospel of St. John.

" Poor fellow, he's left all alone now," said the kindly, if somewhat careless, old Rector to his curate on the day after Obed's funeral. " You might go and see him, Crewe; he seems a steady sort of young man. Perhaps he would like to be asked to teach in the Sunday-school."

Mr. Crewe went on his mission, and was civilly received, but he wished afterwards that he had not taken the Rector's hint and spoken about the school; for his proposition was received in a somewhat singular way.

" Teach!" said Gideon, with a short, sharp laugh. " Do you know whom you're asking? Do you know that I nearly killed a man not long ago, and tried to commit suicide directly afterwards? Is that the sort of teacher the Rector would like in his schools?"

Mr. Crewe was not a ready speaker, and stammered out something incoherent to the effect that Gideon's mind had probably been unhinged just at that time by his great troubles.

"Nay," said Gideon, looking at him with his dark, sorrowful eyes, which Mr. Crewe had some difficulty in forgetting when he got outside the house; "don't you believe it, sir. It's the fashion to say a man's out of his mind when he tries to kill himself, or even when he kills another man; but it isn't always true. It wasn't true with me. I knew what I was doing well enough. The devil had possession of me, body and soul. I hope he's been driven out. But God knows I'm not fit to teach religion to innocent little children; they're much more likely to be able to teach me."

"Anyone who feels as deeply on these subjects as you do——"

"I don't feel anything in particular," said Gideon. "I only know the facts. I'm not fit to teach anybody—that is all; I only wish I were."

"You come to church, don't you?" said Mr. Crewe, whom Gideon puzzled exceedingly.

"Yes," said Gideon slowly, "I come to church;

and—if I may say a word—it seems to me we don't get enough said to us about the evil in our own hearts, Mr. Crewe. Perhaps if we'd heard more about it, some of us might have—*understood* without such—such hard lessons."

His voice broke suddenly. He had said more than he had meant to say, and was ashamed of it, with the natural recoil on itself of a reserved nature; and also he thought of Emmy. She had once played at being a teacher in the school over which Mr. Crewe presided on Sunday afternoons. What good had come of her teaching, he wondered, to teacher or to taught?

Mr. Crewe retired from the scene, half offended, half confused; but he was a man of considerable sincerity, and he said, long afterwards, that nobody had ever influenced his sermons more than Gideon Blake. He fell into the way of preaching to the melancholy dark eyes that haunted him from a corner of the dim old church; and if by chance he made them light up, he went home with a warmer feeling at his heart. He had helped one of his hearers, at least; he had spoken to *one* person who cared to understand.

Gideon's own ideas were very indistinct at this time. He could not shake off a terrible depression, a horrible sense of wrong-doing and misery, which made life a burden. He prayed for help and comfort as he had seen others pray; but prayer brought him no relief. He was as one wandering in the dark, with nobody to show him the way.

On Easter Sunday, it occurred to him to walk to the cemetery and see the graves of his uncle and his little son. He chose an hour when he thought that few visitors were likely to be there, and he was relieved to see that the cemetery looked almost deserted, although it was quite a popular place of resort on Sunday afternoons. One solitary woman's figure in black could be seen at some little distance from the spot which Gideon wished to visit, and that was all.

Someone had been before him. The graves were strewn with white flowers, placed in the form of a cross on each green mound. Gideon wondered, and thought that perhaps Carry was kinder than she seemed. But these flowers were more beautiful than any that grew in Casterby gardens.

As he mused and marvelled, feeling vaguely

soothed by their sweetness, the quiet figure in black passed by him, paused, and passed again. He raised his eyes; they fell on the pale, sweet face of the woman who had once been George Hamilton's betrothed—who had been almost as much wronged by him as Gideon himself had been. He started, and felt his face grow hot, and hoped, with a dull anger at his heart, that she would walk on without speaking to him; but, instead of that, she came nearer, and stood on the other side of John's little green grave.

"May I speak to you?" she said, in that sweet voice which still had the power of thrilling Gideon's nerves.

Gideon hastily and nervously raised his hat, but he could not speak Her presence recalled some cruel memories.

"I came here to say good-bye; it is for the last time," said Frances Lisle. "I wanted very much to see you before I went away. I think God must have sent you in answer to my prayers."

"You are going away?" said Gideon, stupidly enough.

"Yes; I am going to Belgium." Her eyes,

16

wistfully sweet, wandered to the furthest limit of the horizon, and remained fixed for a few minutes on the distant line of low-lying purple hills. "I am going to be a nun."

"A nun?" said Gideon, starting back with the horror he had been taught to feel for women's religious houses. "Why should you be a nun?"

"Why not?" she said, her eyes coming back to his face with a gentle, serious look. "It is the most beautiful life. But I know you do not understand. Only I shall never, most likely, see you again; and I wanted so much to say one thing to you before I went. May I say it now?"

"Yes—anything."

"That is kind. It is not much that I have to say, but it is hard to say it, too. Mr. Blake—some day you may be asked to forgive those who have—who have wronged you——"

"Forgive!" cried Gideon. There was passion in his tone.

"I was wronged, too. I have forgiven," she said, looking him full in the face with her great gray eyes. He noticed how large they looked, how small and pathetic was the worn, white face, how patient the droop of her sweet curved lips, and he knew that even his suffering had not been bitterer than hers. "That is partly why I am going into a convent. I hope to pray for him there—to pray for his soul."

Gideon was silent; it was not possible for him, he told himself, to understand.

"We can forgive in different ways," said Frances, catching at the reason for his silence. "I in my own way, you in yours. But some day you must—you *must*——"

"I shall not hurt him again, if you mean that," said Gideon in measured tones. "I tried to punish him once; he is safe from that now. I know very well that if I had killed him I should have been a miserable man."

"But more than that is necessary," said the girl, in a strangely moved voice. "When I laid those flowers on your little boy's grave, I prayed that I might see you again, but not that I might plead with you for George Hamilton's life! I knew *that* was safe. I want more than that—for your boy's sake, and because you hope to see him again one day. You do not belong to the Church, but you hope—you want to see your boy again?"

"God knows——" Gideon began, and then stopped short. He could not go on.

"I plead for John's sake, then," said Frances Lisle. "And I plead for God's sake, Who cannot forgive us if we do not forgive. You remember what our dear Lord said upon the cross? 'Forgive them, for they know not what they do.' That is what I say every day, every hour of my life: 'They know not what they do; forgive them, Lord, as we—as *we*—forgive.'"

"They are safe—from me," said Gideon, and turned away his face.

"Are they safe from your hatred—from your bitterness of heart? Oh, I know how hard it is! I have no right to speak. But if one could turn one's own pain into an atonement for their sin; if one could weep for them and pray for them until their hearts were touched, they knew not why, and they turned to God and asked Him for that forgiveness which He never grudges to those that ask —then would not even our grief and suffering have been a paradise? The greater the suffering for us, the greater the grace for them!" cried Frances, her face shining with the ecstasy of a vision that she deemed divine.

"Could that happen?" said Gideon, half sadly, half sceptically. "I have read that no man can give his soul for another, or make atonement to God for him."

"But you would do it if you could for one you loved?" said the girl, in a hushed voice.

"Ay, if I could," said Gideon, looking down at the flowers on John's grave.

"That is forgiveness," said Frances. She held out her hand. "I must go now. They are waiting for me at the gate. Good-bye, Mr. Blake. I shall always remember you—and those that you love. And in your heart you have forgiven—or will forgive; I am quite sure of that."

Gideon held her hand for a moment, but he could not say good-bye. He watched her down the pathway until she was out of sight; then he knelt down by his boy's grave.

She did not know it, but she had transfigured the world for him. Into his empty heart she had put a living seed. Forgiveness, prayer—were these

such mighty forces? Then he had something to
live for still; he could love and forgive and pray.

There came back to him the history that he had
heard read out in church on Good Friday; he had
not been touched by it then, he remembered, but it
touched him now. The Man of Sorrows who hung
bleeding and naked on a Cross, jeered at by the
people whom He died to save, could still say,
" Father, forgive them, for they know not what
they do." He was the Great Example: could not
even His humblest follower do something of the
same kind?

Gideon's mind was very simple, very literal, in
some ways. The thing that seemed true to him
must be put into action if it were to continue true.
He could, after a great struggle of heart, after an
agonizing conflict between his natural emotions and
his will, say to himself that he forgave his erring
wife, and even, in some sense, the man who had
led her astray; but how could that forgiveness be
brought into action in his daily life? He could not
seek Emmy out and beg her to return to him; his
common-sense told him that this mode of behaviour
would be impracticable. She had gone abroad;

she was probably happy in the evil of her life—
triumphing, perhaps, in the way in which her husband had been befooled. He could do nothing
directly for her benefit.

But—"to turn one's pain into an atonement for
their sin"! to pray until the sinners were forced
into repentance! Could this be done? Ah, it was
worth trying, thought Gideon, with a great break-
ing-up of all the fountains of his soul: for what
harm would it do even if it were worthless?—and
if it should avail anything—ah, what infinite gain!

His religious views, his notions of heaven and
hell, were what the modern world agrees to call
primitive and crude. He believed in a material
hell, to which he saw himself hastening in the past,
arrested by something like a miracle upon its very
brink, whither Emmy was hastening now. Could
he stop her? Could he by any exertion, any sacri-
fice, save her from the fires of hell? Nothing
would be too hard for him to do, if only he could
"touch the arm that moves the world" and bring
its exquisite, irresistible, compelling power to bear
on Emmy's heart. Emmy's frivolous little prefer-
ences, Emmy's hard little personality, were for-

gotten, absorbed in a great rush of love for what lay behind the shell-like exterior. A soul to be saved—a beautiful, precious, immortal soul: Emmy was that, and Gideon could not hate and despise her any more, although she had betrayed him, and outraged her womanhood, and thrown away her woman's purity.

The thought that he could help her changed his life. It became henceforth, most emphatically, a life made up of prayer. It had already been the life of an anchorite. Now, as soon as his work was over, Gideon hastened to shut himself up in his lonely house and expend the long hours in supplication for Emmy's soul. A roughly-fashioned crucifix hung on the wall in the bare room he occupied. On the floor before it he knelt or lay for hours, praying with tears and cries that Emmy might be saved from the evil to come. Thence it was a short step to more stringent and more painful measures. The passion of penance took possession of his soul—for his own sins partly, but chiefly for those of the woman that he loved. And for her sake he suffered in the flesh as in the spirit— for Emmy's sin.

The world would have called him mad. His own little world of sordid commercialism; the Rector's comfortable, easy-going Christianity; the would-be intellectualism of the Unitarian meeting-house—all would have joined in condemning him. Perhaps even Father O'Brien, with whom, although he did not know it, Gideon was most in sympathy, would have shaken his head dubiously over the young man's vagaries. "For it is not," as Thomas à Kempis says, "it is not after the way of man—to fly honours, to be willing to suffer reproaches, to despise self and choose to be despised, and to desire no prosperity in this world." And it is not according to most men's taste to fast as Gideon did, to tear his flesh by scourges, to wear strange contrivances of wire and cord which took the place of the hair shirt which he had never seen, to conceal a heavy chain about his waist, and to bear cold and discomfort and bodily pain with a wonderful endurance which came less from the thought that there was merit for himself in what he did, than a possible expiation for Emmy's wrong-doing, a forestalling of Emmy's repentance for her sin.

Morbid and mad the modern world would call

him, yet not unhappy, even when the reddened scourge dropped from his nerveless fingers, and he lay at night with bare and bleeding shoulders before the cross, breathing out shuddering, agonized prayers—for Emmy—into the silent night. Yes, it was all for her. That thought gave ecstasy to every pang of pain. And for himself—why, he was ready to suffer an eternity of woe if he could but purchase heaven for her. It was a heathen conception of his God's requirements, perhaps, and one not recognised exactly by any form of faith; but it kept Gideon Blake from misery. And he did not think of the dead priest whose nature he had in some odd way inherited, as we all inherit from unknown generations of the dead, nor ever figure to himself that there had once been a man of his name and his blood who also agonized for his soul and the souls of others before the cross, and who—happier than Gideon—breathed out his last prayer amid the flames that sealed a martyrdom.

Gideon, obeying the law of his own nature, thought nothing of the law of heredity. If he had found no way of suffering for Emmy, or thinking that he suffered for her, he would have gone out of his mind completely. But self-sacrifice, even of the most fantastic kind, consoled him, and steadied his whole nature. He could not be utterly miserable when he could pray and suffer for her sake.

And thus the years went by.

X.

"Let no man dream but that I love thee still."

Joseph Blake was becoming more and more invalided by rheumatism—that scourge of all who lived for many years at Casterby—and greater responsibilities therefore rested on Gideon's shoulders. In spite of the absorption of one side of his nature in purely spiritual matters, Gideon was by no means a bad man of business; he was certainly not enterprising, but he was conscientious and hard-working, and it was well known that anything he undertook would be faithfully carried out. His father had once been afraid that Gideon was of too impracticable a temper to succeed as a master of other men; but of late years, as the change in his character became manifest, it was found that Gideon was liked as well as respected. He was scrupulously just; he was strict indeed, but he was fair, and in times of trouble generous; he never lost his

temper, although he could say a word of keen
reproof now and then, and he set the example of
unfailing industry and punctuality. Joseph Blake
triumphed a little over his wife in pointing out
Gideon's virtues to her.

"They used to call him a black sheep," he said.
"Who's got a son like him in Casterby, I'd like to
know?"

"I've nothing to say against Gideon," responded Mrs. Blake; "but I must say I think he's
very queer. He's that unsociable—you never can
get him to go anywhere or take a cup of tea or anything. If I'd been him, I would have got a divorce
from that wretched woman and married some nice
girl, and had a family round me by this time."

"Gideon don't hold with divorce," said Joseph
doubtfully. "I heard him say so just after it all
happened. 'I'd never feel but what Emmy was
my wife,' he said, and wouldn't hear of anything
else."

"He's very odd in his notions," said Mrs. Blake,
tossing her head. "I think he's got a tile loose, as
people say. For my part, I think it's sheer crazi-
ness to be so religious."

And the world mostly agreed with her.

If he had not been such an excellent man of business, Gideon would certainly have been pronounced a little mad by his fellow-townsmen. He did not talk about his religious faith, nor about his vigils, and fastings, and penances; but rumours of them got abroad, as rumours will get abroad in little country towns. They made him a remarkable person in the eyes of the Casterby people, one of whom strange things were to be expected at any moment. There was a little suspicion of him, even as a business man, and if he had shown one sign of over-cleverness, or given one hint of a speculative turn, he would have lost ground at once and completely in their opinion of him. But Gideon was so steadily humdrum and commonplace in his way of conducting his business, so absolutely without a spice of the adventurous, so content to plod along the common way, that he won approval and considerable confidence from his father's friends.

There was a sale of timber in the North, which Joseph Blake had been anxious to attend; but he was too lame to attempt the journey when the date drew near. Gideon had to go in his father's stead.

The young man accepted the charge of the trans-
action with his usual gravity and habit of attention
to details; he listened carefully to all the instruc-
tions his father gave him, and Joseph Blake knew
that they would all be most conscientiously carried
out. But for once he grew a little impatient with
Gideon. "The lad," as he still called him, showed
no real interest in the matter.

"Your heart ain't in this business, Gid," he said
reproachfully. "I wish you'd waken up a bit."

Gideon gave a slight start.

"Don't I satisfy you, father?"

"Eh, lad, you're as good as goold. But the
spring's gone out of you. At your age, I'd ha'
thought of putting on my best coat, and having a
good time at York. I don't grudge the money.
Go to the best inn, have a smoke and a chat with
the travellers, see the world a bit and enjoy thyself.
It would hearten me up again to see thee do it."

"But—I shouldn't enjoy it, father," said Gideon
with scrupulous gentleness.

"That's the worst of it. Why shouldn't you?
I don't think much of your religion if it makes thee
so gloomy, lad."

Gideon stood looking at his father, as if uncertain what to reply. Joe Blake stared back at him, with a vague sense of uneasiness and inarticulate sympathy. He noticed that his son's great frame was gaunt and thin; that his cheeks and temples had fallen into hollows, and that his bent eyebrows seemed to betoken suffering. And yet he knew that Gideon was not ill. He could do twice as much work as any man in the yard; his strength had increased, not diminished, of late years. But there was the stamp of pain upon his face, and an unutterable sadness in his eyes.

"It's not religion that makes me gloomy," said Gideon, at last, making an effort over himself. "It's the thought of—other things."

"Ay, ay! that's all very well, Gid. But you can't save a bad woman by fretting about her."

Gideon put out his hand. "Don't say things against her, father. It cuts too deep."

"Eh, does it hurt still, my lad?" said Joe Blake, in a half-pitying, half-deprecatory tone. "You've had a mort o' trouble over a worthless lass. But there, I'll say no more. It's just this—

that a trouble like yours didn't ought to be the be-all and end-all of your life."

Gideon raised his heavy eyes to his father's face. " I'd give the whole of my life if it would do her any good," he said.

" Ay, but it won't," said his father rather sharp-ly. "It's wasting your youth and strength for naught."

"Nay, not for naught," said Gideon, turning away, "so long as there's a God in heaven."

He seldom said so much, and his father grunted out a "Well, well, well!" as if he wanted to put an end to the conversation. But Gideon had not done. When once his tongue was loosed, there was a good deal that he could say.

" She's a poor lost soul, I know," he said, in the deep tones which could be soft as well as deep when he was greatly moved—"a lost lamb, straying on the mountains, where nobody can go after her nor find her but the blessed Lord Himself. Do you think I can leave off beseeching Him to find her and bring her home, until it's done? There's not much room in the world for joy and pleasure to me while she is still astray. I can never forget that I cared

17

for her: I care for her still. And there's no rest
for me, no happiness, as the world counts happiness, until she's found."

" Do you mean you'd bring her back to Casterby ?" gasped Joe Blake, in consternation.

" I don't know," said Gideon slowly, " as I'd
ever thought of ways and means. I leave those to
God. If ever the time comes, I shall be told what
to do."

He went away, leaving his father still shaking
his head over these extraordinary notions. Joseph
Blake was troubled for a day or two with the
thought that they must needs unfit his son for the
ordinary affairs of life, and that business would be
badly performed in consequence. But he found no
evidence of carelessness or incompetence in the
work which Gideon undertook to manage about
that time.

The journey to York was made, and the business performed. Gideon stayed three days and
nights, and took the express back to Retford,
whence he could easily return to Casterby. About
half-way to Retford, as he was sitting in one corner
of a third-class railway carriage, looking quietly out

at the brown and yellow tints of the landscape—for
it was autumn again, and the leaves were dropping
from the trees—the accident happened which thrilled
the country from end to end, and filled the newspapers with harrowing accounts of the injuries inflicted and the agonies suffered by the survivors.
But Gideon escaped unhurt.

It happened very swiftly, very suddenly. There
was scarcely time for fear, before it was practically
all over. Another train ran straight into the express, cutting some of the carriages into bits, scald-
ing the engineers to death, setting fire to the frag-
ments of the train. Night was beginning to fall,
and the gathering darkness added to the horrors of
the scene. Gideon, with other passengers who were
not hurt, set to work gallantly to extricate the injured and to extinguish the flames. But their task
was dangerous and difficult, and some time elapsed
before medical assistance could be procured and the
sufferers conveyed to the nearest hospital.

Gideon toiled like a giant and a hero. His
heart was rent by the sights he saw, by the cries of
agony that he heard, but the pity of it spurred him
on to almost superhuman exertions. In one or two

cases, even his great strength would not avail to free some poor creatures from the crushing mass of wood and iron that pinned them down to agony and death, and all he could do was to breathe a prayer into the ear of the victims, and solemnly commend a passing soul to God, before turning away to help those who could be helped. He forgot his reserve, his self-consciousness, in a scene of this kind. Other men looked at him with wonder and admiration, even where all were brave and strong; women and children called to him for help, as if they knew that the weak ones of the earth had the first claim with him. It was amongst the third-class carriages that there was most to be done, for there had been a merry-making of some kind at Grantham, and dozens of country folk were returning to their homes by the afternoon train. But when most of these had been disposed of, Gideon thought that he heard a cry from the wreck of a first-class carriage a little further down the line, and he turned instinctively to look—and help.

"For God's sake, come here!" an imperative man's voice demanded. "Nobody's been here yet. I shall be killed before I can be got out! I'll give you twenty pounds to get me out—I can't stir a limb!"

He sank back with a groan of pain.

"Are you hurt much, sir?" said Gideon, approaching him.

"My leg's broken, I think, and my side seems hurt; but if you could get me out of here, I might feel better. I heard them say that the express might come up at any moment."

"Oh, we'll get you out of here before that happens," said Gideon. "Besides there are men stationed along the line here to stop the express."

"But the fire is breaking out again," said the passenger anxiously. "Look—over there! Can you move that piece of wood? Why didn't you come before?"

He spoke as if he had a right to command, but Gideon took no notice. The man was in pain, and he was frightened, too. Indeed, his position had been one of considerable danger, for he was near the smouldering engine, and jets of steam and flying cinders had excited his fears to frenzy.

"Is there no one else to help," he said. "You can't do it alone."

" I think I can.   The other men are busy."

He bent down and applied his great strength to the fallen mass of wood which lay across the passenger's limbs.   A jet of flame, suddenly springing up from the smouldering débris close by, threw a lurid red light across the scene.   Then, for the first time, Gideon saw the passenger's face. The voice had told him nothing, for it was altered with fear and pain, but the face was unmistakable.

Human nature is strong in a man even after years of repression and conflict.   Gideon stopped in his work.   He had not yet moved the heavy load, but he drew back and raised himself erect without making any further effort.   The movement was purely instinctive—it was natural to him to shrink back from George Hamilton—but it looked as though he had relinquished all intention of helping him.   George Hamilton thought so, as the red light flashed on Gideon's gesture of repugnance and withdrawal.   But he did not recognise the face.

" Damn you, why don't you move it ?" he broke out savagely.   " You're strong enough ; are you afraid ? You said there was plenty of time ; why don't you make haste ? "

" You have forgotten me," said Gideon quietly. " You knew me once, Captain Hamilton."

Then the man saw and understood. He uttered a sharp cry of terror, and struggled vainly to free himself from the detaining load.

" Help ! Will nobody help ? " he shouted as loudly as he could. But his voice was too weak to be heard at any distance, and Gideon stood above him, a giant figure in the lurid gloom, blocking the way. " You villain ! you want to be my death ! You tried to kill me once ; are you going to try it again ? " Then, changing his tone, " Heavens, man, do you see the flame creeping this way ? Do you want me to be roasted alive before your eyes ? "

No, Gideon did not want that. But he felt strongly impelled to walk away and give the wretched man full three minutes of misery until he could send other people to his help. It was far from him to condemn even his worst enemy to such a death as the one that crept nearer every moment to the fallen man. But the old hatred leaped out like a wild beast, and Gideon knew in his heart that he would sooner cut off his right arm than use it to save George Hamilton.

It was a keen temptation. Not to kill him, but to refrain from rescuing him with his own hands—that was all. For a moment he asked himself why *he* should be called upon to save George Hamilton's worthless, wicked life?

But it was for a moment only. The swift recoil of repentance followed instantly. He turned back and threw his whole strength into an attempt to move the weight. Hamilton watched his movements with pallid face and shrinking eyes. He was not sure whether Gideon Blake did not mean to beat his brains out where he lay.

The flame crept nearer. Hamilton could feel its hot breath on his face—it almost singed his hair. But the great weight stirred, moved, was driven back, and then he fainted and knew not how he was drawn away, nor how the succour came to him only just in time.

When he recovered consciousness he was lying on the ground at some little distance from the scene of the accident, and Gideon was holding brandy to his lips. He swallowed a little, and looked round him somewhat fearfully.

"You are quite safe," said Gideon. "They have gone for a stretcher to carry you to the cottage hospital at X——. The doctors will look after you there. They asked me to wait with you till the men came back."

He spoke in short, grave sentences, as if saying only what duty required, and then became silent. Hamilton looked at him with questioning, awe-stricken eyes.

"You—you have saved my life, I suppose," he said awkwardly.

"I tried to take it once," was Gideon's slow reply.

"If I can do anything for you—any recompense —any——"

"I think you had better say no more. You must know it is not possible for me to take anything from you."

Hamilton groaned, and turned away his face. Perhaps he came nearer to repentance at that moment than at any other of his life.

"Tell me one thing," said Gideon, in a low, hurried voice. "She was not with you?"

"Good heavens, no! I haven't seen her for two years."

"Where is she?"

"I don't know."

"What, have you left her to starve?" said Gideon, in a stern, passionless voice. "After ruining her life—and mine, did you turn her out into the streets?"

"She left me of her own accord—I swear she did," Hamilton answered eagerly. "If I knew where she was, I would tell you—though I don't suppose it would give you any satisfaction to know."

He glanced at Gideon's face; it was very pale, and the lips were quivering. Hamilton felt a pang of shamed regret.

"I—I'm very sorry I can't tell you more," he stammered out.

"God forgive you," said Gideon, turning aside. He could say no more. "God forgive me, too," he added to himself.

His very love for his wife, his hopes, his fears, his struggles, made it hard for him to speak to the man who had compassed her shame and his misery.

Yes, he had saved his enemy's life, but his strength failed him to do more. Later, on the heights of a self-abnegation which was almost sublime, he blamed himself for not saying more, for not making some effort to bring home to Hamilton's heart the truths for which he himself was ready to lay down his life. But just then he had done as much as he was capable of doing,—and it was more than most men would have done.

Hamilton was carried away to the hospital, and Gideon occupied himself for the rest of the night in ministering to the hurts of those who were less seriously injured, but still required care. In the early morning he heard that one of the railway porters was inquiring for him, and he went out of the cottage where he had been tenderly nursing a child whose back was hurt, and found a man waiting for him at the door. It was one of the men who had carried Captain Hamilton away.

"You're the chap as pulled the gentleman out, ain't you? He's sent you this, mate," said the porter, thrusting a note into Gideon's hand.

Gideon looked at it with distrust. "What is it?" he asked.

"Dunno. A five-pun note, mebbe. Open it and see," as Gideon made a movement as if to give it back. "Law bless you, I don't know what 'tis."

Gideon opened the letter. To his relief, it contained no money, nothing but a few words scrawled in pencil on a half-sheet of paper:

"Miss Violet Leslie,
191, *Coleman Street,*
Westminster,
London, W.
"*Try this address.—G. H.*"

Gideon stood looking at the paper. What did it mean? His mind, dazed with excitement and want of sleep, did not move quickly. Who was Miss Violet Leslie? And why should he try that address?

"Nothing but a word o' thanks, I s'pose," said the porter. "Them 'igh chaps is sometimes raight down mean. He moight ha' been burnt to a cinder if you hadn't come along in time. Doctor says it's nobbut a broken leg and a rib or two, and he'll soon put him straight."

"All right; thanks," said Gideon, turning away. He went back to the child, who was already crying out for his strong arms, and he sat and nursed her until she was taken away in a cab to the nearest town by her father. Her mother had been killed in the accident.

When he had done all that was required of him, and a good deal more (including a narrative of the accident to a reporter, who published it that evening with a number of sensational additions of his own composition), Gideon tramped to the next station and took train for Retford and Casterby. He was shocked to see his father waiting at the station, haggard and trembling, and scanning every face at the windows as he sought news of his son.

Gideon jumped out. "Father, I'm all right. I'm here."

"Thank God!—I thought you might be hurt, Gideon."

"I was a fool not to telegraph. But I never thought you would hear so soon, and I was busy helping the other folk."

"I'll be bound you were. And you're not hurt?"

"Not a scratch. But I'm black as a coal."

He was certainly very grimy, and walked stiffly

from fatigue; but there was more alacrity in his air, more light in his eye, than usual. He looked as if some new hope had come to life within him.

Old Joe Blake put it down to the stimulus of danger, and looked at him with admiring wonderment.

Gideon stumbled down to his house and went to bed. In spite of his excitement, bodily fatigue made him sleep for some hours at a stretch; and when he woke up, it was to find himself famous, or at all events popular, for the first time in Casterby.

He had never given his name, and did not consider that his deeds were worthy of record; but, as it happened, he was known by the officials on the line, and "Mr. Gideon Blake's great strength and marvellous courage" had been chronicled by the ubiquitous reporter, and been transmitted to every paper in the country, much to the satisfaction of Casterby and the confounding of Gideon himself. People turned to shake hands with him in the street, and to ask him details of his adventure. He told them that he had only done what any other man would have done, and tried to break away from their congratulatory looks and words; but the fact remained that many of the rescued passengers owed life or limb to his strength and his endurance, and were not slow in rendering him the tribute of their gratitude. He devoutly hoped that Hamilton at least would say nothing about their meeting; but even this could not be kept a secret, although the story did not creep into the newspapers.

"What's this about Hamilton, Gid?" said his father to him a day or two after his return.

Gideon's pale face flushed.

"What do you mean?" he said, frowning a little, though not angrily.

"There was someone of that name in the accident. Was it—the same?"

Gideon nodded.

"They say *you* saved him. Was that so?"

Gideon was silent for a moment.

"If I did, it was after a delay that might have cost him his life and made me a murderer after all," he broke forth almost defiantly. "It was no credit to me. Don't speak of it, father, if you please."

"No credit to him!" muttered the old man, as

he watched Gideon cross the yard and begin to use his tools again with an energy which showed that he did not wish to be questioned. "No credit to him to save the life of a man who has injured him in that way, does he say? Well, I don't think I could have done it myself—I don't think I could."

The story got wind in Casterby, but it was received in different ways. Some people thought that, as Gideon had said, it did him no credit. It seemed a work of supererogation for him to be the one to save his enemy's life. Why had he not let some other person do it? Miss Lethbury opined that it was hardly decent. And there was a general feeling that to love one's enemies was somewhat poor-spirited, and that it would have been more natural and reasonable if Gideon had let Captain Hamilton alone. An act of virtue like that made ordinary people feel quite small.

A week elapsed before Gideon sought his father again.

"Could you spare me for a few days?" he asked, with unusual abruptness.

"Spare you? Where are you going, lad?"

"I want to go to London," said Gideon, avoiding his father's eye.

Joseph Blake pondered; then he looked up at his stalwart son, and noticed that his very lips were pale.

"You've heard—something, Gideon?"

"I don't know," said Gideon desperately—"I don't know what it means. I may be going on a fool's errand; but, for God's sake, don't hinder me, father! I must go."

"You wouldn't—you wouldn't—be for bringing her back—here, Gideon?"

"I should have to find her first. I can't tell. But I must go to London."

"Can't you tell me what you have heard, boy?"

"No, I can't; I don't understand it myself. But I must satisfy my own mind. I've been putting it off for days; I did not know whether I could do any good. But it seems to me that that's not my business; it's my duty to go."

"Then go, lad," said Joseph Blake kindly; "I won't hinder thee. But I doubt whether you can do any good."

"Say 'God bless you,' father, before I go."

18

"God bless you, my lad! Do you want to go
at once?"

"To-night," said Gideon, with trembling lips.

But his eyes were steady and clear.

The old man blessed him again, and said good-
bye.

Then Gideon went home and put his things
together. He was going to catch the train that had
borne him to London once before, but with what a
different purpose in his heart! For then he had
been full of bitterness, and strong in his desire of
vengeance; but now love and compassion ruled the
day. And it seemed to him that he had done wrong
in not going earlier to look for Emmy; but he had
never thought of seeking her in the flinty-hearted
London streets.

The little house by the river looked very gloomy
and desolate as he turned the key in the front-door
and put it in his pocket, for he was to leave it with
Keziah, who lived in a house which he would pass
on his way to the station. It always had a desolate
look in autumn, when the rains had been coming
down, and the river had overflowed its banks and
stood level with the garden-beds. The floods had

been out again, Gideon remembered, and he wondered for a moment whether his house were safe.
His father had spoken to him about the foundations
not long before. "I suppose it will last my day,"
he said to himself, glancing back at it with a sort of
sad affection as he closed the garden-gate. He had
an impression that his "day" was not likely to be
long. Not that he thought of death for himself, but
he sometimes contemplated leaving Casterby when
his father was no longer living. It sometimes
seemed to him that there was a larger life into
which he might enter in another place. He might
work as well as pray. But if he could only find
Emmy first! . . .

XI

" Love seeketh not itself to please,
Nor for itself hath any care."

GIDEON reached London before dawn, and em-
ployed his leisure time in finding a room for himself, and in breakfasting. After breakfast he sallied
forth to Coleman Street, Westminster, although he
had a very dim idea as to the reason of his expedi-
tion. He had concluded in his own mind that Miss
Violet Leslie was one of Emmy's friends, and that
she had information to give him. He was surprised, however, to find the house a squalid-looking
place, with " Apartments to Let " in the window.
A red-faced, bare-armed landlady, in a gown that
did not meet across her chest, answered his question
with a burst of abuse.

" Yes, I know Miss Vi'let ; who doesn't ? " she
said, when her wrath had calmed down a little. " A
nice lot she is, and does credit to her friends ! No,

she *ain't* here, and I wouldn't 'ave her in my 'ouse again for huntold gold."

"Can you tell me where she is gone, then?" said Gideon entreatingly.

"No, I can't. You'd better look for her along Piccadilly; you'll find her there most likely," said the woman with an insulting laugh.

"Piccadilly?" said Gideon hesitatingly.

"You silly lout! don't you know where Piccadilly is? You'll soon find out. Go there to-night and look; you're pretty sure to see Miss Vi'let Leslie, as she calls herself—no more Miss Vi'let Leslie than I am."

"Do you know a Mrs. Blake?" said Gideon, not yet discouraged. "I think she is, perhaps, a friend of Miss Leslie's."

"You're from the country, I take it. You don't know much about London, young man, that's plain. Is Miss Leslie a friend of yourn?"

"I never saw her in my life. But Mrs. Blake——"

"I don't know no Mrs. Blakes. But Vi'let Leslie—anybody 'll p'int her out to you if you go to Piccadilly Circus at ten or eleven o'clock to-night.   All the girls knows her, an' the p'leecemen, too.   Ask a p'leeceman, young man ; he'll tell you where Vi'let Leslie's to be found."

And she shut the door in his face.

Gideon knew very little of the world.   But he knew evil from good, and had seen something of both, even in a country town.   In Casterby, however, evil did not flaunt itself on the pavements, and smile at the passers-by from under the flaring lamps.

He found himself at Piccadilly Circus between ten and eleven o'clock, watching the crowded pavements with troubled, wondering eyes.   Girls with bold eyes and painted faces laughed at him over their shoulders, and made jokes at his expense; he was so manifestly unaccustomed to the scene that he was fair game.   Some of them spoke to him, or passed him with a flick of their floating boas, a whisk of their silken and embroidered skirts.

"You poor child," said Gideon to one of them, who was a little thing not more than sixteen or seventeen years old, "go home, for God's sake, and ask Him to deliver you from evil!"

He got a jeer and a laugh for his pains, and

for some little time afterwards he heard his own words passed with loud, half-drunken laughter from mouth to mouth, as if they were the most amusing thing he could have said.

"Have I come down into hell?" asked Gideon of himself.

The streets were as light as day; the restaurants were crowded; men in evening dress were coming out of the theatres, and walking slowly along the pavement. The road was crowded with cabs and omnibuses; the cries of the omnibus conductors mingled with the loud laughter of the girls and women who walked arm-in-arm round the corners, hurrying a little lest they should be hustled by the police. Others stood motionless in corners, as if half courting, half dreading observation. Now and then a respectable woman hastened anxiously, with eyes set straight before her, lest she should see something she did not want to see, towards cab or omnibus, or a couple of Salvation Army lasses came past with *War Crys* in their hands. Once or twice a "Christian worker"—Gideon instinctively recognised the type—tried to speak to a loiterer, who generally responded by a broad smile and a meaningless nod of the much-curled and befeathered head. Gideon felt himself lost, alone, in the midst of a crowd of human beings whose bodies alone were living, whose souls were dead.

A big policeman had·been keeping his eye upon him for some time, and now accosted him with asperity.

" Move on, young man," he said, "if you're not waiting for a omnibus ; move on, please."

Gideon turned and looked at him. The man had a sensible, honest face.

" Look here," said Gideon ; "I was told you would know a—a lady called Miss Violet Leslie, and if I asked you, you would point her out to me."

" Don't know any such person," said the policeman stolidly.

" I don't know her either," said Gideon, "but I've lost my wife, and I believe Miss Leslie can tell me where she is."

Policeman X. cast a sharp glance at Gideon's face, and his stern brow relaxed a little.

" I think I know the party you mean," he said cautiously, "and she's generally out o' the theatre

by this time.   If you stand 'ere for a minute or two
I might be able to tell you which she was.   She's
one of the worst o' the lot.   I wouldn't 'ave any-
think to do with her, if I was you.   You're from
the country, ain't you?"

"Yes," said Gideon, wondering how people
found it out.

"So I thought from the cut of you.   Now, you
take my advice, and go 'ome again.   This ain't the
plice for you."

"It's as much my place as that of most of the
human beings I see," said Gideon, with a dreary smile.

The policeman looked at him solemnly.   He did
not understand.

"You've never been 'ere before, have you?
Well, the less you see of it, the better."   He was
quite paternal to Gideon.   "As for Miss Leslie,
she's a chorus lady, you know; the less you see of
her, the better, too."

"Indeed!"

"She's what they call good-looking," said the
man critically, "and I don't say that she drinks as
much as some of 'em.   There she goes!   See her?
The party in the white hat."

Gideon looked. "The party in the white hat" was a very pretty girl, who came laughing up the street with a number of companions, mostly young men. She was very fashionably and beautifully dressed; her cheeks were rouged, and her golden hair was elaborately curled almost to her darkened eyebrows. But her eyes, those blue, still innocent-looking, appealing eyes! They were Emmy's eyes.

"There she is," said the policeman, thinking from Gideon's silence that he had not heard. "That's Miss Violet Leslie, of the Comedy——"

"Nay, you're wrong," said Gideon, in deep, indignant tones. "It's no Miss Leslie—it's my wife."

And he plunged forward, regardless of consequences, facing the girl as she came laughing and singing up the street.

"Emmy!" he said.

She stopped short. It could be seen that she turned white beneath her paint, and that a look of fear and shame came into her beautiful eyes. He held out his arms to her; but with a shriek that was half of laughter, half of fear, she put her hands up to her face and fled, as if for dear life, across the crowded road. Gideon tried to follow her, but was pulled back by his friend the policeman, otherwise he would have been somewhat roughly handled by the men and women who called themselves Emmy's friends.

"Lord love yer! what was you thinking of to do a thing like that?" said the policeman. "You'd have been run over in another minute, and set upon by those young chaps as soon as you got into a quiet street. What was you saying—that you knew her?"

"I said that she was—my wife," said Gideon, gasping for breath.

"Once, maybe," said the policeman cynically. "I'd not call her my wife now, if I was you. You go back to the country and leave Miss Leslie to take care of herself. She's on the boards, and doing fairly well; but she's as bad as they makes 'em, so I'm told."

"I must see her again. Where shall I find her?" Gideon said, not heeding the admonition.

"She won't come 'ere again for a bit; or, if she does, she'll maybe ask me about you. Shall I take your address? Or you might leave a note for her at the box-office of the Comedy. Then she can write to you if she likes."

Gideon thanked his adviser, and, in spite of his warnings, crossed the road and sought the turning which he fancied Emmy might have taken previously. But he saw nothing more of her. Too much excited to go home to bed, he roamed the streets for hours, seeing the signs of revelry die away, to be succeeded by the stillness of night and the desolation of the dawn. He thought of that other night, part of which he had spent so miserably upon the Embankment and Blackfriars Bridge. It was hardly more wretched, more hopeless, than was this.

He could not think; he could not even pray. The old yearning for Emmy's love, long suppressed, long ignored, had come back to him, mingled with the pain of his new knowledge. What could he do to save her? Perhaps she would refuse to see him, to speak to him, and what then could be done? But he would never leave her; he would haunt her steps, night and day, until she promised to come home again.

But she was not quite so obdurate as she had

seemed. He wrote his note to her, imploring her to grant him an interview; and in return he got a line written in the flowing, rather illegible handwriting that he knew so well: "You may come to see me if you like. Ask for Miss Leslie." Then followed the address—a house in a little slum leading out of Regent Street—and, by way of signature, a single initial: "E."

He started off for the house as soon as he received the note, without the slightest notion that he might not be welcome at eleven o'clock in the morning. He was kept waiting in a dirty passage, where the paper was peeling off the walls in unhealthy-looking patches, for some minutes; and then requested by a grimy little servant-girl to walk up to the second floor, as Miss Leslie would be there directly.

Gideon went upstairs. It was a foggy day, and the house smelt close, although the air outside was raw and cold. At the top of the second flight of stairs he saw an open door, and concluded that he was to enter. It was a sitting-room, shabbily furnished, but adorned with cheap Japanese fans, and art muslin which had grown filthy to the eye and clammy to the touch. The remains of a meal partly covered one table, which was also littered with gloves, a dirty handkerchief or two, a brush and comb, and a powder-pot. On the mantelpiece he saw curling-tongs, and cold cream, and other articles of toilet; also some photographs of theatrical-looking persons, and a sticky medicine-bottle, labelled " The Mixture—as before." One or two dresses were thrown over the chairs, and a comic paper lay open on the floor.

Gideon regarded the dirt and disorder of the room with the feeling of one in a horrible dream. He had bought some flowers as he came along, with the faint hope that they might recall to Emmy's mind the innocent pleasures of her earlier life, and show her also that he came not as an enemy, but a friend. The poor tea-roses, with their exquisite fragrance and bronze-green leaves, looked out of place in the tawdry surroundings of Emmy's London room. Gideon was half sorry that he had brought them. He laid them on the table beside the powder-pot, and turned to see Emmy enter by the folding-doors from the room beyond.

He saw now that she was older. There was no

paint on her face, and there were dark shades below her eyes, and plainly-marked lines round her mouth. And there was the curious look, half bold, half shy, only seen on the faces of those who have known what it is to be ashamed. Gideon would have recognised that look if he had been in the habit of frequenting Piccadilly at midnight.

Emmy was in a dressing-gown of pale blue, with a falling collar of Breton lace—not very clean—at her neck, and frills of the same at her pretty, slender wrists. She was very graceful, as she had always been; and her hair was uncurled and hung in soft waves over her forehead, much as it had done in the days when Gideon had wooed and won her at Casterby. She was not so much changed after all, he thought; only she was always laughing —giggling, he might have called it—as she had never laughed at Casterby. Perhaps the laughter came from nervousness. She held out one slight hand, and laughed when Gideon touched it.

"You're not much altered," she said. There was an indescribable hardness and boldness in her tone. "But you're handsomer, you know. I don't think I ever noticed that you were such a fine man, Gideon."

The dark face that was turned to her had a fineness which had been gained during the ordeal caused by her own falsity. It had been sharpened and refined to beauty; while in hers, once so lovely, certain lines of weakness and sensuality had marred the loveliness beyond hope of recovery. Yet to Gideon she was as beautiful as ever.

"Emmy! Why did you run away from me the other night?" he asked.

She shrank a little.

"Don't call me Emmy," she said; "it makes me feel inclined to cry. Nobody calls me Emmy now. I'm Violet—Violet Leslie, of the Comedy. Won't you come and hear me sing some night, Gideon? I always had a nice voice, you know."

"I'm here to ask you to come back to me, Emmy."

"What rubbish!" she said, laughing shrilly. "As if I should ever dream of such a thing! Besides, you don't want me——"

"I've wanted you every hour since you went away."

"You have John—your beloved John. How is he, by the way?" said Emmy, tossing up her chin.

"Emmy, don't you know? He died three days after you went away."

"Oh! I didn't know."

She stopped laughing, and bit her lip. Gideon went on:

"He was asking for you all the time he was ill. You would make him well, he said. He——"

"Poor little fellow! It gives me the blues to hear you talk, Gideon. You're just the same as ever. I've had another since then," she said, laughing a little wildly. "He died, poor mite! I was rather glad he died. I believe he's buried at Highgate Cemetery. His name was Gerald Hamilton: I always liked Gerald for a name."

The pain in Gideon's face seemed to touch her for a moment.

"Gideon, you're an old silly!" she said. "I'm not your wife now, and you needn't look at me like that. I'm nobody's wife, thank goodness. I'm a free woman now. What lovely roses! did you bring them for me? Awfully nice; I'll wear them

19

at the theatre this very night, and tell everybody you gave them me."

She stopped short suddenly. There was a new look on Gideon's face. She remembered it in anger; she did not remember it in this transfiguration of pity and of love.

"Emmy," said the deep, gentle voice, "you are my wife still. My dear, I have not forgotten. As long as I live I shall never let you go. In the sight of God we shall always be man and wife. And I love you, dear—I love you as my own soul. Emmy, cannot you love me again and come back to me?"

She was impressionable, easily swayed, and the tears started to her eyes as she listened to him. But she answered impatiently:

"Of course I can't, Gideon. It's an impossibility."

"Nothing is impossible, Emmy."

"Nonsense! It would never do. What *would* your people say?"

"They should not have the chance of saying anything. We need not live at Casterby. I would do anything you liked. We might go to some new country where we should not be known. I would give my life to make you happy, if only you would give up this—this life of yours, Emmy, and come home to me."

"So easy!" she said, with another little toss. "I'm not good, you know; I'm bad. Everybody says so. A real, downright bad un. That's what they call me: 'an old offender,' you know. That's in the police courts: I've been there ever so many times. What do you think of that?"

"Emmy, I'll kneel to you to ask you to give it up and come with me. It will not be so difficult to be good, dear. God will help you. And the way you are going leads to death and despair—and hell. I can't bear to think of it. Can't you leave it—for *my* sake? How could I bear to see you a lost, ruined creature, when you might be safe and happy and good? I love you too much to bear it, Emmy: come back to me."

He knelt at her feet, and, catching her hands in his own, pressed them to his lips. Emmy resisted a moment, then burst into a passion of tears, and snatched her hands away.

"It's not only me that loves you, Emmy," said

Gideon, now fairly embarked on the pleading words
that he had longed to utter. "The Lord, who sent
me to you and helped me to find you, He loves
you, too. He doesn't want you to perish . . .
poor lamb! . . . I love you, but He loves you
more. You can't bear to disappoint us, Emmy—
we that have waited all this time for you to come
back again . . . the lost sheep on the mountains
. . . lost and found again."

His words were broken by sobs; he knelt still,
although she had withdrawn herself from his
clasp; and she, crying too, was keenly conscious of
every word he uttered. Suddenly he broke forth
into prayer—the cry of a heart for which the finite
was too narrow, which only an Infinite Love could
satisfy.

"Lord, save Thy child! Lord, give her grace
to come back to Thee. Thou hast loved her all
the while, and I have loved her too. She belongs
to us, Lord: she is Thine and she is mine. Let
her come back to us. Let her know how much we
love her, and what that love of ours can do for
her, if she will. Lord, her child is in heaven with
Thee—her children. . . . Shall she not see them

again ? Thou knowest how one of them called for her. He is calling for her still. Send her not, O Lord, into the place of darkness, but bring her back to Thyself . . . and John . . . and me."

His voice failed him suddenly. He bowed his head, and could say no more. But as he prayed in silence, there came soft arms round his neck, and a sobbing voice at his ear:

"I will come, Gideon . . . I wanted to come . . . If you can only forgive me and love me still . . . I will try to be good again."

XII.

"And I shall claim thee mine before High God!"

THE first step—the rush of love and shame and penitence—seemed easy enough; what followed was more difficult.

Emmy shrank back after that first reconciliation. She was a volatile creature, easily elated, easily depressed. Anyone but Gideon would have found her vacillations, her uncertain temper, her fits of waywardness and wounded vanity, unbearably trying. But Gideon put up with everything.

It was as if all the labour, and toil, and pain of his youth had gone to the production of this one beautiful flower of a perfect love. It was a love that defied anger and coldness and contempt; that flourished on the very unkindness of the Beloved; that wrapped the Beloved round as with a garment, as with the very loving-kindness of God. It was a love that did not shrink from going down into the gutter to seek for the precious thing that had been lost. And such a love, the consummation of a life-time, the fine issue of a spirit finely touched, is sure to meet with its reward.

As soon as the stress of emotion had passed by, Emmy began to make objections to everything Gideon proposed. She declared that she could not break her engagement at the theatre without a heavy forfeit. This Gideon undertook to pay. Then she said that she was in debt to her landlady, who would detain her boxes if she could not settle the arrears of rent. Gideon summoned the landlady, and paid up every penny. Then there were things (which she *must* have) to get out of pawn. These Gideon sent the landlady to procure for her. Then she sulked and raved against her fate, and especially the fate that was taking her back to Casterby. But Gideon was very gentle with her, and after a time she melted into tears again and acknowledged herself very wicked, and begged him to forgive her, and declared that she *would* try to be good. She was more like a spoilt child than a woman, and if Gideon had not possessed a wonderful faith in that supernatural power on which he relied, he would have stood aghast at the light irresponsibility of her nature, and the difficulty of making upon it any impression which would last more than half an hour.

He dared not leave her alone; he felt that she might run off and leave him, in a fit of desperation, at any moment. His only chance lay in getting her out of London as quickly as possible. And in one of her quieter moods, he told her his plans for her.

"I want you to come home with me just for a day or two," he said. "You need not see anybody unless you wish. But I should like to go and collect a few of my things, and there are some things of yours, and of John's, dear, that I thought you might care to take. I would get my money, and we would start as soon as you liked for another country. I have often thought that I should do pretty well in Australia."

"It wouldn't be bad," said Emmy encouragingly. "Yes, I shouldn't mind that; but I could not live at Casterby."

"You should not live at Casterby, dear. You would be happier in a place where there was more to see and hear. Nobody would know us in Melbourne or Sydney; we could begin our lives afresh."

She looked at him with eyes that had grown thoughtful and pathetic.

" Yes, nobody would know," she repeated. " It would be easier there."

" We could be happy together, Emmy."

" Could we ?" she said, with a little hysterical laugh. Then she came to him and put her arms round his neck as she stood behind his chair. " Who taught you to be so good, Gideon ? You weren't like this in the old days, you know."

" Forgive me for those old days, then, dear."

" Forgive you ? Forgive *you !* Oh, Gideon, you are a saint. I don't know what to do with you, you are so good. And I've never—never "—beginning to weep passionately—" never asked you if you could forgive *me.*"

" Yes, dearest, you did. And that is all over now."

But she cried, and would not easily be comforted.

It was in this softened mood that he got her at

last to start for Casterby. He would not have chosen to go back if he could have thought of any other way of managing matters; but he felt that he must see his father before leaving the country, and he dared not leave Emmy alone, and he knew no friend with whom he could leave her even for a day.

As they neared Casterby—which he had arranged to reach at nightfall—she grew scared and anxious, pulling down her veil and shrinking back into a corner of the carriage.

"You don't think we shall see anyone? You don't think anyone will know me?" she asked her husband.

He sat beside her, holding her cold hand in his own, and trying to console and encourage her by every means in his power. He had telegraphed for a fly to meet him at the station, for he remembered the times when she had grumbled at the walk home through the sloppy streets. It was raining, as usual; it seemed always to rain at Casterby.

Emmy shivered as she saw the drops upon the pane.

"I'm afraid you are very cold," said Gideon,

with solicitude. "Shall we go to the Rose and Crown instead of our own house? You would be more comfortable at the hotel."

"No," said Emmy; "I'd rather go home. Somebody would be sure to know me at the hotel, and I could not bear being looked at and talked about."

"You would not be known, perhaps, if you kept your veil down," said Gideon, a little hesitatingly.

"No, I want to go home. I've a sort of idea that I should like to see the house again—and John's things," she said, with a touch of shyness and sadness which gave a new reality to her words. "You don't mind taking me there, Gideon, do you?"

"I was only afraid it would be desolate for you, dear. Let us go home, then," said Gideon, quietly.

He had telegraphed to Keziah to put the place in order for his home-coming, but not to stay in the house.

Emmy half repented her choice when the fly set them down at the head of the dark lane leading to the little house by the river. The rain fell at intervals, and the wind was wild and cold.

In the passing light which came from a glimpse of the moon when the clouds broke now and then, she could see that the fields were under water, and that the river looked wide and high.

The flyman gave Gideon a warning as he was paid.

"Floods is out again," he said. "They say them houses down theer bean't very safe."

"Oh they're all right," said Gideon cheerfully.

He had no fear for himself, and he did not want to frighten Emmy. If matters looked bad they could easily go to the Rose and Crown after all. He gave her his arm as they walked down the lane. He could hear the hysteric catch in her breath as he pushed open the little creaking gate. The path was very wet to their feet; in fact the garden seemed half under water, and there were pools at the very door of the house.

But indoors all was light and cheerfulness. In obedience to Gideon's orders by telegraph, Keziah had wonderingly lighted fires in the chief rooms of the house, and left lamps burning, and an ample meal set out on the kitchen table. Gideon's instinct told him that the kitchen, with its shining brass and tin, its red-brick floor and high black mantelpiece, was the most home-like room in the house. Not yet could he bear to sit in the green rep parlour, where he had watched beside John's dying bed and wept over John's little coffin before it was taken from his sight. He put his wife in the cushioned rocking-chair, which had once belonged to Uncle Obed, and himself took off her boots and her cloak, waiting upon her with a gentleness, an assiduity, which startled Emmy into quietude.

Indeed, she was very quiet. The atmosphere of the old house, the sight of familiar objects, seemed to subdue her. She did not laugh any more, but looked at Gideon wistfully as he moved about the room.

"Where's Uncle Obed?" she asked suddenly.

"He is dead, Emmy."

She shivered again.

"I declare I'm afraid to ask after anybody. Is your father——"

"He's all right. He is rather infirm, that is all. I don't think anyone else has died in our families—only those, you know."

"Mother——"

"She lives just where she did, and the children are all growing up."

"Do they—do they know—about me?"

He came to her side and laid his hand on her shoulder; his silence told her that they knew.

"It's very hard," said Emmy, weeping. "Every-one thinks so badly of a woman—like me, and I'm sure I'm not worse than other people. I suppose mother wouldn't like me even to go near the house, nor speak to Mary and Jenny if I met them in the street?"

Again Gideon was silent for a little while, hardly knowing what to say.

"My dear," he said at length, "you know there is joy in the presence of the angels of God over one sinner that repenteth——"

"I know I'm a sinner; I've been told so often enough," said Emmy. "But whether I repent or not——"

She twisted her handkerchief nervously between her fingers, and looked into the fire.

"We can talk afterwards," said Gideon, think-ing it better to change the subject. "Come and eat something; I've made the coffee, and here's cold meat and cakes and things. Or would you rather have tea ? ”

“ I think I’d rather have brandy,” said Emmy, with a reckless laugh. “ Tea ?—wish-wash ! Well, give me the coffee, if you’ve nothing else in the house. I suppose you don’t drink whisky now as you used to do ? ”

“ The coffee is better for you,” said her husband adroitly. “ Drink it, and eat something, then you’ll feel better.”

She did as he suggested, but her appetite soon failed her. She sat with her hands in her lap, listening to the wind with a far-away look in her blue eyes.

“ How the wind howls ! ” she said at length. “ Well, it’s more comfortable here than walking the streets in London, any way. I’ve stopped out all night sometimes—hadn’t anywhere to go, you know. I used to think of you, safe and warm here with Jacky. I did not know that he was gone, of course. I didn’t think of you being all alone.” She paused a little and reflected. “ Uncle Obed gone, too ! Have you been living here all the time by your-self ? ”

"Yes. Since Uncle Obed died—three years ago."

"And you never thought of getting a divorce and marrying again? You could have done, you know."

"Not as long as I loved you, my dear."

Emmy laughed, with a sob in her throat.

"I never saw anyone like you," she said. "I'd no idea you cared for me like that. I never believed in a man being faithful and true. Gideon, it makes everything much worse that you've loved me all this time."

"Why worse, dear?"

"It makes me seem worse to myself. I often got tired of it all, and wished myself back in Casterby. But I thought you'd turn me from your door if I came back."

"Never, Emmy, never! So long as our Lord has not turned *me* away, how could I think of shutting you out of my heart?"

"I don't understand all that," she said. Then her face softened and her eyes filled. "I only understand how you've cared for me; and I've only *you* left now."

"The rest will come in time," said Gideon patiently. It was something that Emmy should understand his love.

Presently she said something about going upstairs, and he took her to the room which she had occupied in the old days, where John's crib still stood between the white-curtained bed and the wall. Keziah had understood that a visitor was coming, and she had left a fire burning, and aired the white sheets that smelt of lavender, and drawn the chintz curtains close over the window. The room looked almost as dainty as when Emmy had first went away. Gideon left her there alone.

"It's quite pretty," said Emmy to herself, looking round. "It's all just the same—just the same. He hasn't changed a thing. Nothing's changed, except—except me. And John has gone—oh, it would be much easier if John were here!"

For the loneliness and silence of the place tried her nerves. She was used to the noise and bustle and glare—she called it "life"—of the London streets. What could she do with Gideon, here, alone? Her heart sank. And yet—yet—she wanted to be "good," as she phrased it. If only

20

she could stand the dulness of life alone with him!

Away from her, Gideon had gone into that poor, plain little room with the truckle-bed and single wooden chair, which he had used since his return from London after John's death. He looked round it with the feeling of a monk on some enforced renunciation, some inevitable return to the ordinary world. The rudely-carved crucifix, made by his own hands, hung on the wall; upon the floor beneath it lay a knotted scourge. Gideon picked it up and put it out of sight. He knew that this phase of his experience was over. There would be no time now for midnight vigils and scourgings and penitential tears. He would have other work to do. His penance would consist in the laborious attempt to teach and turn another soul to good. It was a boon, a blessing, an answer to his prayers; but he dimly felt that it would be a penance, too.

He knelt and said a prayer for Emmy—hardly for himself, save in an incidental way. Emmy's state absorbed him far more than his own. He would willingly have bartered his hopes of eternal happiness for an assurance of hers, if such an ex-

change had been possible. It seemed to him as
though he had acquired new rights over her soul, as
if he could now compel her to be "good."

After a time he knocked at Emmy's door. He
was afraid of leaving her too long alone. She
looked up from an open wardrobe at which she was
standing as he entered, and he saw what she held
in her hand. It was a pair of John's shoes; John's
toys were ranged upon the shelf before her, and his
little clothes were piled in rows in an open drawer.
She turned round with tears upon her face. Gideon came up to her, and put his arm round her slender waist.

"Ah, thank God that you are home again!" he
said passionately.

She laid the shoes down, and turned to him, and,
with a quick, impetuous movement, threw herself
upon his breast.

"Oh," she said, "I *am* sorry; I do repent,
Gideon, I do—but only because you love me. I
should never have come back, if it had not been
you that sought me out. But I'm not worth it—
not worth your love—not worth the love of anybody in the world!"

She sank down before him, her head touching the ground, her hands clinging to his feet, sobbing, broken, exhausted. The memorials of her child had brought her to herself. Gideon tried to raise her; but at first she would not yield to his touch, but dragged herself away from him, and sobbed with her face upon the floor.

"I can't bear it that you should be so good to me," she said. And after another interval: "I will do anything you like. I will try to be a good wife to you—if you will take me back, and if I live; but I think—now—I could die—die of my shame."

After a time he raised her up and drew her close to him, speaking comforting words; and then, according to his simple creed and rule, he prayed aloud for her and for their future life.

"It may be hard," he said to her later, as he sat by the fire, and she crouched at his side with his hand upon her neck, "but we must bear the hardness for a time. We all have to pay. When we have sinned, it is the sin itself that punishes."

"You haven't never sinned," she murmured, touching his knee with her hand.

" Millions of times, Emmy."

" But not—not as I have," said Emmy, with her fair head bowed against his knee.

" Oh, my dear!" he cried, out of the depths of his passionate love, "what does it matter which of us it was? We were one flesh. When you went astray, it seemed to me that I went, too. I prayed God to let me take your punishment upon myself. I suffered with you, and for you, all the time."

" *For* me?"

" I put on sackcloth; I chastened myself with fasting; I laid your guilt upon my soul. Child, if you had gone to hell, I must have gone too! I felt that you could not die alone."

" Oh, Gideon," she said, "you make me afraid!"

" Afraid of what, my dear? You would not go back to the old bad life again?"

" I would die first," she said.

He drew a long breath. Was she not given back to him, body and soul, for this world and the next? It was well to have lived—well to have wept and prayed and agonized—for this supreme deliverance, for the glory of this hour!

"What is that?" she cried at last, lifting her head.

The storm had risen to a gale; the wind howled round the house, shaking it to its foundations. They had heard a strange noise—a crack, an ominous rending sound. The walls quivered before their eyes. Gideon sprang to his feet.

"The house is not safe," he said. "The river must be rising. Let us go, dearest, while there is time."

They gained the head of the stairs. Then Gideon put his arms round his wife, and strained her face down upon his breast.

"Don't look," he said. "Don't be afraid. Emmy, we shall never be divided any more—thank God!"

And the rain descended, and the floods came, and the winds blew, and beat upon that house; and it fell. And great was the fall of it. For beneath its ruins, when daylight came, the seekers found Emmy and Gideon, clasped in each other's arms.

THE END.

www.ingramcontent.com/pod-product-compliance
Lightning Source LLC
Chambersburg PA
CBHW031402270326
41929CB00010BA/1295